Time of Trial

Time of Trial

Rhona Prime
with Jean Watson

HODDER AND STOUGHTON
LONDON SYDNEY AUCKLAND TORONTO

British Library Cataloguing in Publication Data

Prime, Rhona
  Time of trial. — (Hodder Christian paperbacks)
  1. Prime, Geoffrey Arthur
  2. Espionage, Russian – Great Britain
  I. Title   II. Watson, Jean
  327.1′2′0924   UB271.R92P7

ISBN 0 340 36141 7

I wish to dedicate this book to my dear husband, Geoff, and to my three special sons, Mark, Stephen and Craig.

My aim has been to tell the truth as I see it and I hope that through what I have written many hurts will be healed.

I would especially like to thank those members of my family and all the friends who have supported us in so many ways, as well as those who have been involved in the writing or production of our story – in particular Jean.

Contents

Time of Trial

1

Geoff

On an unforgettable day in spring, I went into our bedroom to find my husband, Geoff, sitting in his favourite crosslegged position on a rug on the floor and staring into space. I tried talking to him but he answered abruptly. His withdrawn morose attitude and the mixture of heartache, frustration and annoyance they aroused in me were all too familiar at that time, but then, as I was making for the door, he suddenly looked at me and said, in quite a different tone, 'If ever I go, am gone, or am missing, just remember the good times, Rhona.'

His words brought piercing anguish and the dread certainty that something terrible was going to happen soon and that it would involve my husband going or being taken away.

But why, and when, and where, and for how long – I had no idea.

Now, knowing the answers to those questions and thinking back over the five years of our marriage prior to April 27th, 1982, I do remember the good times.

I remember how Geoff brought hope and kindness into my life when we were both at a very low ebb, physically and emotionally – his first marriage having already ended in divorce, and mine, to Peter, going very badly wrong.

Peter and I had had financial as well as other problems and to ease the strain in that area, we had been taking in lodgers. Geoffrey Prime had been our second one – coming to us straight from London, where he'd been working as a

Russian linguist with the Government Services in London for eight years, and about to take up similar duties at Cheltenham's Government Communications Headquarters – usually referred to as GCHQ. Prior to that he had served with the RAF in various places, including Berlin and Kenya.

I remember feeling drawn to this very shy, sad-faced man. We were rather different in temperament – he being a man of few words, a solitary individual, rather inclined to be moody and over-anxious; I tending to be more sociable, easygoing and optimistic. But we became more aware of these things later. At first, I believe, both having experienced the trauma of a failed or failing marriage, we felt sympathy for and tried to help one another. For my part, I was grateful for the kindness he showed to us as a family while my divorce from Peter was going through.

I remember, too, the gradual growth of our friendship and my amazement when Geoff asked me to marry him. It seemed miraculous that anyone would be willing to assume responsibility for me and my three sons, then aged ten, nine and four.

We were married in June 1977 and I recall the tremendous relief I felt when Geoff became head of the household, paying the bills and helping with the upbringing of the children – who didn't always appreciate his strictness but grew to like and respect him as a person.

I look back on Geoff taking us on family outings; playing football with the boys; talking about world affairs with Mark; watching matches and discussing sport with Stephen; buying for Craig (and spending hours helping him to use) an aid specially designed for children with reading and spelling problems; taking me out to meals or, more often, to see foreign films, particularly Russian ones.

I recollect how, right up to the last few months and despite his own problems, my husband worked hard at uncongenial jobs in order to give us a good home and comfortable standard of living; how he tended the garden, with Craig as a willing assistant.

Yes, with pleasure and gratitude, I remember the good times.

But there were sad, perplexing times, too.

I cannot forget Geoff's abrupt resignation, only three months after our marriage, from his good, well-paid, pensionable job at GCHQ; or the day when, without saying anything to me beforehand, he almost left us to go and live in the Soviet Union – an action which brought home to me shatteringly the extent of my husband's admiration for that country and its people, culture and political system.

Nor can I blot out the memory of the two occasions when he went away for a few days – each time soon after we had had a phone call from a foreign-sounding gentleman, about whom my husband had said nothing. Instead he gave me what I felt were puzzling or implausible explanations for his trips: the first being that he had to go to Vienna to collect and deliver a car to a friend; the second that he needed a break between jobs, and for this he went, allegedly, to Wales.

I remember the shock and bewilderment I experienced because of these odd occurrences and the suspicion to which they gave rise – one so incredible and unacceptable that I tried to push it and the incidents out of my mind and immerse myself in the business of being both a working mother and housewife.

With hindsight, I can see that our differing political views were a source of tension between us. Soviet Socialism, Geoff believed, though not yet perfect, was moving towards the ideal of fairer shares and fairer deals for all. I shared his sympathy for the underdogs in society and his anger at social injustices, but I had to part company with him over the solution to these problems and had no desire to live in the Soviet Union. Having worked at GCHQ, Geoff would not have been given clearance to go and live there – hence his attempt to defect: a plan he had abandoned because of his feelings for me and the boys. But having come back to us, there were other problems.

I recall the agony of seeing my husband lapse into periods of deep unhappiness and the frustration of not being able to find out what the matter was, let alone help him or get him help. All he'd say was, 'You don't know the half of it, Rhona.' I well remember how those words, previously dismissed as an infuriating catchphrase, rang ominously in my ears one day; how I puzzled, fearfully, about the other half that I did not know, wondering whether it accounted for my husband's inability to relax, his tendency to worry compulsively over one thing or another and his depression. These characteristics became more marked as time passed.

My thoughts go back to the worst time of all when Geoff seemed to be totally withdrawn and locked in despair. He uncharacteristically neglected the bills and other household matters and, on some days, instead of going out to work, sat in our room for hour after hour. Even when he did leave the house, I wondered how he could possibly do a job in the state he was in.

I remember agonising over what I should do, in view of the gloomy – even oppressive – atmosphere in our home and the fact that I was becoming a rather tense, preoccupied 'mum' and wife, and that Geoff, far from benefiting from the close relationships of marriage and family life, as I'd hoped that he would, seemed increasingly unable to cope with them.

Reluctantly, painfully, I reached a decision but, before I was able to tell my husband that I felt we ought to separate for the time being anyway, he became suddenly attentive and affectionate again and we began to communicate better than we had been doing for a long time.

My resolution melted away. Despite all the shadows which had fallen across our relationship, we had grown, I believed, to love and respect one another. Building on this, we could surely sort out our problems – one of these being work. Since leaving GCHQ, Geoff had been a taxi driver – a job which had not worked out well – and then a wine salesman, a position not suited to his reserved temperament. The next priority, I felt, was finding a job which would prove satisfying and suitable for my husband. Because of his interest in and knowledge of the wine business an idea took shape.

I remember how we both latched on to this scheme of

owning and managing a wine shop in or near Cheltenham or Gloucester and how we discussed details with Mr Davies, our solicitor, and approached a wine company, the manager of which said he'd be willing to consider us for one of his retail outlets. While waiting for our dream to become a reality Geoff read up all he could on the subject and made the decision to hand in his wine salesman's job and find some other means of earning a living for the time being.

After five chequered years, we were still together and we cared for one another. With signs of an improvement in Geoff's state of mind, and a project to plan and work for together, our future course, I believed, promised to be brighter.

And then, on April 27th, 1982, everything changed.

2

Prelude

The morning of April 27th began much as usual with Geoff up, dressed, and down to breakfast first, followed fairly soon by Mark, then aged fifteen, and rather later and more sleepily by me and my two younger sons – Stephen, aged fourteen, and Craig, nine.

We three arrived at the bottom of the stairs just as Geoff was about to leave for Bristol to terminate his job with the wine company which had been employing him. I wondered whether he'd be feeling relief at the prospect of finishing with work he'd hated, or apprehension about the future, or both. But his face gave nothing away as brief goodbyes were said, before he left the house and Stephen, Craig and I went and joined Mark at the kitchen table.

Breakfast over, the two older boys cycled off to their school – the local grammar – and Craig set off a few moments later to pick up a lift to St Mary's Infant and Junior School, where I worked as a cook-supervisor. After doing a few chores, I cycled to work, glad that the weather was fine and bright.

I liked my job and there was usually a good-humoured atmosphere among the staff. All morning we prepared and cooked the food and then at lunch time pushed trolleys laden with liver and baked beans – or 'cowboy hot-pot' as we preferred to call it – to the tables of chattering children. When the meal was finished we cleared away.

Afterwards, at about three o'clock, I cycled home, then flew about preparing the evening meal until it was time to

14

hop on my bicycle again and make for the centre of Cheltenham and the driving school where I was enrolled as a new
and very nervous learner. Having survived the lesson I did a
quick shop for groceries. Then I loaded the shopping bags on
to my cycle, which I pushed along beside me as I headed for
home on foot.

Past the shops and down the high street I walked, my
thoughts turning to my family and the evening ahead. There
was the meal to cook and some cleaning and clearing to be
done. Mark and Stephen would no doubt have homework to
do. Perhaps after tea I'd give my parents a ring as I hadn't
seen them for a day or two.

And then I thought about Geoff and the job situation. I
knew he could always resume work as a taxi driver, but
perhaps he'd prefer something else. Hopefully, whatever he
did decide to do would only be temporary employment until
the plans for our proposed wine shop materialised. When they
did Geoff could manage the business and I could help him
and perhaps in the future organise snacks as a sideline . . .

I had almost reached the turning leading into our rather
narrow lane when I was met by Stephen and Craig.

'Oh, hullo boys,' I said, pleased if a little surprised to see
them.

'The police have been to our house,' they announced.

Instantly alarmed, I demanded, 'What do you mean – the
police have been to our house?'

'They came to see Geoff,' Stephen told me.

Immediately assuming that the visit had had something
to do with driving, I felt reassured. The boys didn't seem
worried, either, so their coming to meet me, I decided, must
have sprung from a childlike wish to share their news with
'mum' as quickly as possible.

We walked the rest of the way to our detached chalet-style
house with its cream-coloured walls and dark wooden front
door. Stephen and Craig went straight through the hall and
kitchen and out into the back garden. Mark, I expected,
would be in a little later and perhaps go upstairs to get on
with his homework.

I went into our lounge-cum-dining room. Geoff was in there, reading – seated in an easy chair beside the bookcase which held his thirty-volumed Russian encyclopedia, among other books.

'What's all this about the police, then?' I asked casually.

'Oh, they came round in connection with some assault which took place last Wednesday,' he answered lightly, looking up.

'Assault? Good gracious!' I exclaimed, alarmed again.

'It's nothing,' Geoff said calmly. 'They're checking on cars and ours happens to be the same model as the one involved in the case. So they wanted to know where I was last Wednesday. They'll be round later to see whether what you tell them agrees with what I said.'

'That's all right then,' I said, relieved, and went through to the kitchen to cook tea. Geoff followed me and then, typically, sat on the back doorstep gazing out at the garden, which he loved and spent hours working on. It was bright with daffodils, clematis and honeysuckle; and quiet, too, Stephen and Craig having gone round to the front – to play football, I presumed.

The kitchen door was wide open but I didn't mind because the evening was fine and warm. I busied myself at the stove, preparing and then cooking mince, carrots and potatoes.

Geoff's voice broke the silence between us.

'They asked for fingerprints. Do you think I should have agreed?'

Not having been thinking about the police, I was momentarily nonplussed and then surprised.

'Of course you should have!' I said. 'I mean, you're not guilty, so that will just clear your name.'

'Yes, you're probably right,' he said, quietly, then lapsed into silence as I concentrated on the meal.

Suddenly he stood up saying, 'I have to go out now.'

'But the tea will soon be ready,' I protested, feeling surprised and annoyed.

'Sorry, but I have to go out for about an hour,' he insisted. I sensed that it was no use asking why but it occurred to me that he might be going to look at cars. We certainly needed a new one but I wondered how we'd be able to afford it.

'Oh, all right,' I said grudgingly.

He went out and I finished the cooking and called the boys. When the four of us were sitting round the kitchen table someone asked, 'Where's Geoff?'

'He's had to go out – probably something to do with work,' I said.

The boys weren't very talkative but they seemed to enjoy the first course and the rice pudding which followed it. Afterwards they went off to amuse themselves or do homework while I remained in the kitchen, reading the local paper, the *Gloucestershire Echo*.

An hour after my husband had left the house, he returned. Oblivious of the significance of this moment, I merely put down the paper and got up to give him his meal. He was still feeling uncommunicative and ate very little – due to worrying about the work situation, I guessed.

Afterwards, uncharacteristically, he washed up the tea things.

3

The intrusion

As we were finishing the clearing up, the doorbell rang. Geoff went to answer it, and I thought, *The police – what a nuisance!* He opened the door and a moment later a man and a woman stepped into the hall.

'Good evening,' the man said. 'We're from the Hereford Police, investigating an assault which took place last Wednesday.'

Thankful that the boys were out of earshot, I led the way into the lounge. When the four of us were sitting down, the man started questioning me, while his colleague made notes.

'Did your husband pick you up after work last Wednesday?'

'Yes, he did,' I replied.

'Was he late?'

'Yes, but he telephoned earlier to say that he would be.'

The man proceeded to give details of the recent indecent assault on a girl. Horrified, I interposed, 'Do we really have to go into all that?'

'I'm afraid so, Mrs Prime,' he answered apologetically. His colleague gave me a sympathetic look. Geoff's face was expressionless.

The man resumed the story. I felt indignant and tried to turn a deaf ear to the sordid details.

Suddenly the hatch at the dining room end opened and Craig's curious nine-year-old face appeared.

'What are you doing?' he asked.

'Just talking to the police – won't be long,' I answered,

adding, *I hope!* as a fervent afterthought. Craig withdrew and a moment later I heard the back door open and close.

The policeman began to speak of a similar assault which had taken place a year earlier, and for which, they believed, the same man was responsible. I sat still, trying to block out his words and longing for the interview to come to an end.

At last our visitors stood up to leave. Geoff and I went with them out of the front door and into the drive where our brown and cream Ford was parked. When we reached this, the two officers stopped, then proceeded to walk round the vehicle, studying the paintwork and peering in through the windows. Standing by, I felt unnerved by this scrutiny.

They moved off and Geoff and I followed. At the gate I asked, 'How long will this fingerprint business take?'

'Just a few days,' the man replied. 'We'll be in touch – one way or another – quite soon.'

'Thank goodness for that!' I said. Geoff made no comment. The police said goodbye to us both.

'Goodbye and I hope I'll never see you again,' I replied meaningfully, but with a smile to show that nothing personal was intended. They answered in the same vein, 'I'm sure you won't,' then got into their car and drove away.

We turned and walked back towards the house.

'Let's go for a drive,' Geoff suggested. I hesitated but not for long. A quiet drive on a lovely evening sounded very appealing.

'Yes – great,' I said. 'But I must organise the boys first.'

Having seen Craig into bed and left strict instructions for Mark and Stephen to be in charge and put themselves to bed at half-past nine, I got ready to go out.

A few moments later, we were driving up Cleeve Hill, Cheltenham's highest point. Geoff pulled up on a grassy bank near a farm gate flanked by low green hedges. Beyond the gate lay a field of grazing sheep.

Sheep always made me think of Beethoven's *Pastoral Symphony*, the twenty-third psalm and happy holidays in Scotland. I knew that for Geoff – an animal lover, brought up in the country where his father had managed a small-holding –

they evoked many memories, too, and also symbolised peace and contentment: states of mind which he longed for but never experienced.

For a moment or two, I gazed at the peaceful, pastoral scene stretched out before us.

4

Nightmare

Geoff broke the silence between us.

'It's me they want,' he said.

I didn't need to ask who 'they' were but my shocked mind groped for an explanation as to why my husband was wanted by the police. All I could come up with and voice, incredulously, was the old rejected suspicion.

'What – for spying?'

'Oh no, for the girls,' he said.

The words seemed to hang in the air for a few frozen seconds. Then they registered and it was as though the ground had been cut from under my feet and I had dropped straight down into the middle of a nightmare. I felt utterly lost and a painful numbness overcame me. Even so, I became aware of Geoff looking at me and saying, 'Why don't you shout, or scream, or *something*?'

With an effort and in a faint voice I replied, 'I can't, Geoff. There's nothing left in me to do anything like that.'

He laid his head on the steering wheel. I sensed his utter dejection, but could not respond.

A moment later, lifting his head, he said bleakly, 'I know it's wrong but at times the compulsion became too strong for me to control.'

The numbness was getting worse. Geoff asked, 'Do you mind me telling you about it?'

As if from a distance I heard myself reply, 'Oh, no, Geoff, if it helps, carry on.'

Words bottled up long and guiltily came pouring out of him. I couldn't or wouldn't take in much of what he was saying. Either way, it helped me to bear his confession.

Dusk fell over the hill. I felt cold and started to shake.

'We can't stay here,' said Geoff, noticing. 'But I'm afraid I can't face the boys.'

'I'm not sure that I could,' I answered.

'There's a pub in Winchcombe,' he suggested.

He drove down the hill towards the little country village. After parking the car, we went into the pub, where the bright lights and the cheerful, noisy atmosphere jarred horribly. But we needed to fill in time and at least in here we would be warm. He queued for drinks and I found a place to sit down. Geoff, always ultra sensitive to noise, groaned when he joined me and noticed that we were sitting next to a space invaders machine.

'We won't be able to stand this for long,' he said. We sat there – he drinking lager and smoking and I sipping my sherry – thinking our own terrible thoughts. Our occasional small talk struck me as particularly futile.

It must have been half-past nine when I said, 'The boys should be in bed by now.' We left the pub and drove through the now dark and quiet streets.

Home at last! Leaving Geoff in the car I slipped into the house. There was no sign of Mark or Stephen. With a sigh of relief I went to tell Geoff. A moment later we were in the lounge, closing the door behind us.

I got out the brandy and poured a glass for Geoff and one for myself. He drank some, then plunged on with his confession. I listened, guardedly, still partly protected by a feeling of stupor.

After a time it dawned on me that, untypically, I had been drinking fairly steadily while my husband – whose RAF background had taught him to hold his liquor with the best of them – had drunk only a glass.

He stopped talking at last. It was, I noticed, midnight.

With a great effort I asked, 'What are we going to do about all this, Geoff?'

'I'll have to confess to the police in the morning,' he replied.

Then he added, 'And while we're getting everything straight, before I'm taken away – there's something else. You were right. I have been a spy.'

Though this confession was not quite the bolt from the blue which the first one had been, it was nevertheless devastating. Here was my husband actually admitting to espionage!

He continued, 'I worked for the Soviet Union for a long time. I wasn't blackmailed into it and I didn't do it for money. I did it of my own free will for ideological reasons.'

I managed to say, 'I did wonder where the money was coming from – particularly recently.'

'There were never any vast sums – just expenses really,' he told me.

He spoke of how troubled he had been about what he'd been doing and said that his resignation from GCHQ had been his way of finishing with the double life he'd been leading. Since then, however, he had met his Soviet contacts, at their request on two occasions.

Here, I realised, was the explanation for his visit to Vienna two years before and the one supposedly to Wales the previous November.

At the first of the two meetings, Geoff said, he'd told his Soviet contacts that his heart was no longer in the work. They had tried to persuade him to go back into espionage, but he had given them no commitment. At the second meeting, his last with them, they had given him four thousand pounds.

Why such a large sum, I wondered vaguely. Geoff was now saying something about the money being their attempt to induce him to change his mind concerning the decision he had made and to retrain. He added that he had been using it to pay the bills, especially in connection with the car.

Wanting everything cleared up now that the truth was coming out at last, I asked, 'Who was the man with the foreign accent who has telephoned you?'

'I'd rather not tell you any more, Rhona,' he said firmly.

'It's best for you if you don't know too much. In fact, the less you know, the better, just in case you get involved in any way in this in the future.'

It felt like a slap in the face. Just when all the barriers were coming down he'd put them up again! I was hurt and angry but knew it would be pointless to argue. Instead I demanded, 'What if this man tries to contact me when you've been taken away?'

'Say you know nothing,' he said.

For the second time I asked, 'What are we going to do about all this, Geoff?'

'I don't think we need to do anything,' he said. 'I've finished with spying and afterwards we'll be starting a new life together.'

'With all this on our conscience?' I asked.

'We could go and confess to a priest,' he said.

'I couldn't go along with that, Geoff. That wouldn't put everything right.'

He stood up saying, 'I've got to get some sleep now.' As he left the room, I said, 'I'll be up later.'

I sat on, trying to face up to the stupefying revelations I had just heard.

Geoff – a *spy*? The thought had crossed my mind before, but my overriding conviction had been that spies were fictional. There were a few real ones but people like me never ever met them – let alone married them! And even now I wasn't wholly convinced otherwise.

Could most or even all the spying be in Geoff's mind? Tied up in some way with the horrific business with the girls?

Shying away from those details because the pain was too excruciating, I focused on the thought that Geoff's problem would now be contained and, hopefully, dealt with, as I believed he himself wanted.

No wonder he had been so guilt-ridden and desperate!

The brandy hadn't helped me at all. I left the glasses where they were and went, heavy-footed, up the stairs.

Geoff was in bed and appeared to be asleep. I put out the light and undressed in the dark.

A moment later I was lying in bed, confronted by the painful jumble of my thoughts.

Who was this man beside me? Was he the person I knew and loved, or was he the man who had done those terrible things? Evidently he was both, so which was the real Geoff?

My husband stirred and spoke. He had not been asleep after all. Side by side in the dark we talked again – stiffly, defensively at first.

I sensed his total vulnerability and his unspoken question to me. Now that I knew the worst, would I reject him?

Gradually the conviction grew that the man I thought Geoff was and had found him to be, *was* the real person. And that person I could not reject because I still, among all sorts of other feelings, cared about him.

And yet the thought of all the anguish in store for us and all those we loved was unbearable. With all my heart I wished the next day would never dawn.

But the night passed relentlessly by.

5

Phone calls

The dreaded morning came. I woke early, feeling utterly weary. Geoff was awake too. Some of the strain had gone from his face and I sensed that he was relieved at having told me the truth at last. With this new openness between us, we could have started building a better relationship. Instead, the police would be taking my husband away.

I lay flat on my back and tried to think of the horrifying, unknown future.

How long would Geoff be away? How would I cope on my own? What would I tell the boys, and the rest of my family and friends? How would they react? How would others, when our private lives became public news? It was all too over-whelming. I remembered that I was supposed to be getting up soon and going to work. It seemed very unimportant, but I would have to ring the headmistress and tell her some-thing.

I heard the boys going downstairs but I felt incapable of moving, let alone getting up. My head was pounding and my whole body ached.

Beside me Geoff said, 'I'm sorry but I can't face the boys. I'm afraid you'll have to go down and see to them.'

'All right,' I said flatly, making no move. After a time I forced my reluctant body out of bed and into a blue dressing gown – a birthday present from Geoff.

My head pounding more than ever, I made my way downstairs and into the kitchen, where the boys were helping themselves to cereal. Just seeing them brought tears to my eyes and I had to pretend to be very busy at the stove as a cover-up. As I filled the kettle and did the other routine breakfast chores, I was in agony at the thought of what the children might have to suffer.

Mark was quite a mature fifteen year old. I felt sure he had sensed that something was wrong, but he couldn't possibly have any inkling of the true situation. Would he cope?

Then there was Stephen, a year younger – a sociable character as far as friends were concerned but one who found it difficult to talk deeply with his family. Would he be able to share with his friends?

Craig worried me, too. Geoff had been like a father figure to him for more than half of his nine years. How would shy, trusting Craig survive?

All three were well into their breakfasts, so I poured a cup of tea and took it upstairs. Geoff was sitting crosslegged on the bed. He was smoking and his face now looked sombre. I handed him the tea, then sat down near the bedside telephone. I picked up the receiver and dialled St Mary's School. The headmistress answered the call.

'Hullo, this is Rhona Prime,' I said, making an effort to sound as normal as possible. 'I'm afraid I won't be able to get in to work today. I have a stomach upset. I'm sorry.'

'That's all right,' was the equable reply. I replaced the receiver then went downstairs and functioned as usual while the boys finished breakfast and left for school – Mark and Stephen first and Craig a little later.

I went upstairs carrying another cup of tea and sat on the bed. Geoff hadn't moved. He seemed completely wrapped up in his own thoughts. I sipped my tea and cried quietly.

'We ought to ring a solicitor first,' Geoff said.

'Yes,' I agreed.

'Do you think Mr Davies would act for us?'

'Yes,' I said again. After a moment, I reached for the phone book, looked up the number and said it aloud. Still Geoff sat and smoked. The suspense was becoming unbearable. At last he stubbed out his cigarette.

As he dialled the number, the enormity of what we were

about to do hit me afresh. Panic-stricken, I heard my husband say, 'This is Mr Prime. I need to see you straight away.' His next words, after Mr Davies' reply, were, 'Thank you. We'll be round very soon.'

After we'd dressed, I said, without enthusiasm, 'We must eat something.' Together we went downstairs and into the kitchen. I put two slices of bread into the toaster. When the toast popped up, we ate it, mechanically.

Soon afterwards, we were driving through the streets now clear of rush-hour traffic and trying to think about what we would tell Mr Davies. His office was a Regency building at the other end of town just off the famous Cheltenham Promenade with its attractive gardens. But I had eyes for none of these things.

Mr Davies greeted us with his customary politeness. How young and untroubled his face looked! The three of us sat down together in a large airy office.

Geoff asked whether Mr Davies would act for him on an assault charge. I flinched at the word but the solicitor looked unmoved and said that he would. My husband then gave the necessary information – speaking almost clinically, and Mr Davies replied in the same vein.

Part of me felt exasperated at their coolness in the face of this situation but when I spoke I sounded calm too.

On the drive back, I was so overwhelmed by panic that by the time we reached home I barely had the strength to get out of the car and into the house.

Once in the lounge, I sank into a chair. Geoff followed me into the room and then sat down by the phone. He looked up the number of Hereford Police Station and dialled it.

When the call was answered, he asked by name for the detective sergeant who had called on us the previous evening. This man, he was told, was not available, so he was put through to the person in charge of the case – Detective Chief Inspector Smith.

Then my husband said, 'This is Mr Prime of Laburnham Cottage, Cheltenham. I'm calling to confess to the assault charges that I was interviewed about last night.'

Incongruously, I thought about the policeman on the other end of the phone. No doubt he would hardly be able to believe his luck at being handed such a confession!

Then I began to think of what we had set in motion and was stunned and horrified again.

I saw Geoff put the phone down and heard him say that the police would be with us in about an hour.

'An hour?' I echoed aghast. But after forcing myself to think calmly, I saw that this was reasonable, given the distance and the country roads between us and Hereford.

'Let's use some of the time to pay our bills,' Geoff said.

I went to the kitchen, and he to the car – to get some cigarettes, I presumed, but when he joined me, he had a thick wad of notes in his hand.

'There's six hundred pounds here,' he said. 'It's dirty money, but you're going to need it.'

I hesitated, but not for long. The bills which, uncharacteristically, Geoff had not been paying in the past months, had been worrying me for some time, and this would at least clear them up. Life would be enough of a struggle without owing money, I told myself. Aloud I said, 'All right. I don't like using it, but if you're going away, I haven't much choice, really.' I put the money into my handbag.

For the second time that morning, we drove into town. Geoff stopped the car and I forced myself to get out and go through the motions of waiting at desks, handing over money and collecting receipts. Hardly aware of my surroundings, I felt completely cut off from the people around me.

Half an hour later, having somehow managed to pay the mortgage and the heating bills, we were back home again.

Inside the front door, Geoff said, 'I think you'd better come upstairs. There's something I want to show you.'

6

The police

I followed my husband up the stairs and into our bedroom. He went over to the bed, then bent down and reached for something underneath it. When he stood up, I saw that he was holding a white plastic carrier bag. He opened it to show me the contents.

I saw newspaper cuttings and white index-type cards with writing on them. There seemed to be a large number of both.

I was aghast, realising that this was to do with the girls. Then came the question. Why on earth hadn't Geoff destroyed what must surely be evidence against him?

Aloud I asked, 'What are we going to do with all this?'

Standing by the bed, we started to discuss the question. I felt limp and confused, and my impression was that Geoff was feeling the same.

Then I glanced out of the bedroom window just in time to see the top of a black-and-white hat bobbing up and down as its wearer moved closer and closer to our front door. Such timing seemed significant.

The doorbell rang. Geoff pushed the bag under the bed before going downstairs. I followed, then stood behind him as he opened the front door. The blue uniformed policewoman on the doorstep gave us a friendly smile and said, 'I'm from the local police and I've been asked to come and sit with you till the Hereford police arrive.'

Geoff stood aside and she stepped into the hall.

'Are you all right?' she asked.

'How *can* we be all right?' I retorted, in sudden exasperation.

We showed her into the lounge.

'I'll make some coffee,' I said and went into the kitchen. When I reappeared a moment later, Geoff was sitting near the telephone and the policewoman opposite him. I handed each of them a steaming cup, then brought my own in. I drank my coffee while inwardly fuming at her intrusion into what was left of our time together at home, which made it necessary for us to behave as though everything were normal.

She started asking me questions. 'How do you feel about all this, Mrs Prime? . . . Can you cope with it? . . . Are you facing up to it? . . . Do you realise what your husband has done?'

I answered tersely, not understanding at the time the purpose of such questions and resenting their personal nature.

Then she asked, 'Are you going to support him?'

'Yes, I am,' I answered. If Geoff felt reassured to hear this, his face and manner gave no inkling of it.

'That's great!' she responded warmly. 'So often the families reject these people, so they've got nothing.'

It was Geoff's turn to be questioned. How was he feeling? How was he going to cope? . . .

He too kept his answers short.

'You've done the right thing,' the woman assured us. 'This is the only way he'll get help, isn't it?'

She started talking about herself – her work and her plans for getting married. I felt my annoyance melting away. She was so young. How could she possibly understand our situation? How could *anyone*? And after all, she'd only been doing her job and undoubtedly meant well.

The doorbell rang again. Geoff stood up and went out. He returned, followed by a man, then another and another . . . I became alarmed at the number of them – six altogether.

One introduced himself as Detective Chief Inspector Smith from Hereford CID. He looked young and was very smartly dressed. We shook hands with him and then, as he introduced them to us, with each of his colleagues in turn. By the end, I felt thoroughly flustered. The chief inspector proceeded to explain why he and his men had come and what they would all be doing. I couldn't take in all he said, but one thing did penetrate the fog in my mind. When they left, they would take Geoff with them.

Three of the men followed Detective Chief Inspector Smith out of the room and the place felt a little less crowded, but I was still very bemused as Geoff and I and the police-woman sat facing two of the detectives. One, rather well built, was wearing a brown suit.

'There are some questions I need to ask you,' he began. His next words were right out of an Agatha Christie thriller.

'You are not obliged to say anything and I must warn you that anything you do say will be taken down . . .'

I listened, in stunned disbelief, as he went on spelling out the statutory warning that I'd never ever dreamt would be directed at me or anyone I knew and loved.

Then came the questions addressed to Geoff.

'Are you "Mr Williams"?'

'Yes,' was my husband's reply.

'Did you also call yourself a painter and decorator?'

'Yes.'

This was torture. The picture that was emerging was of someone devious and furtive. I couldn't bear it.

Geoff's voice broke in on my quiet sobs.

'Are you all right? Do you want to go out?' I looked across at him. His face was full of concern and there were tears in his eyes.

'I'm all right. I'd rather stay,' I said in a choked voice.

But as the terrible questions continued, I cried even more.

The door opened to reveal the inspector. I made a desperate effort to control myself as he said, 'Mrs Prime, can I ask you to come upstairs and identify your husband's clothes?'

That was too much.

'Surely that's a job for my husband!' I protested.

'No, I'm afraid it's something you have to do,' he said, his tone conveying regret and sympathy.

I rose shakily to my feet and left the room. The inspector followed me up the stairs. I hadn't had time to tidy the bedroom and automatically apologised for the mess.

'Don't worry about *that*, Mrs Prime,' was the reply. Before he finished speaking, I was giving all my attention to what Mr Smith's colleague was doing. He was tying a label round a polythene bag containing an article of clothing. On the bed and on the floor were other similar bags.

The inspector said, 'After the assaults, the girls described various items of clothing and we need your help in identifying these.' Everything in me wanted to recoil in horror from such a task, but the inspector held out one of the bags to me and said, 'One of the girls mentioned a pair of brown trousers. Do you think these would be the ones?'

'How on earth should I know?' I retorted. 'I can't possibly remember what anyone wore several days ago.'

'Just do your best,' he urged kindly. He continued, 'Now, a brown track suit was mentioned. Have you any idea about that?'

Geoff had only one brown track suit. I went and found it and gave it to the inspector. His colleague bagged and labelled it.

The excruciating process went on and on. Shoes, belt, ties, shirts, socks, jumpers . . . I had to try and find or identify everything on the inspector's list, item by item, while for the first time a little of the reality of what had happened to the girls began to register; but it was too painful to dwell on.

I was aware of Mr Smith's sympathy and concern for me. He said, 'This sort of thing is not *so* uncommon. There are people like this or even worse, but they can get help and be sorted out. This way your husband will get the help he needs.'

At last it was over and I could go downstairs. Half-way down, it struck me belatedly that there were strange men all over the house invading our privacy. I knew what they were doing in the lounge and bedroom. But what, I now wondered indignantly, were they doing in the garage?

I went outside to investigate. Two men were making a

thorough search of the place. I asked them, 'What are you doing?'

'Just looking for newspaper cuttings,' was the reply. Recoiling from that thought, I retreated to the house and thence to the lounge.

They had finished questioning Geoff and he now went upstairs to change, accompanied by a policeman.

I sat in the lounge, crying quietly.

Geoff reappeared, wearing a navy blue suit over a shirt I had liked and persuaded him to buy – a red one with a white collar. His expression was taut.

The inspector asked, 'Is there anything else we should take away?'

'There's a bag upstairs,' Geoff replied. Turning to me, he said, 'Could you go and fetch it, please, Rhona?'

Numbly, I obeyed. The inspector took the white carrier bag.

Then he said the dreaded words: 'You'd better get him ready to go.'

7

The parting

I had known that this moment would come. Even so I was thrown into a worse state of shock and confusion.

What would Geoff need, I wondered foggily. The answers eluded me. The inspector suggested a few toilet articles. The bathroom was downstairs next to the kitchen. I went into it and looked vaguely round. It was as much as I could do to remember, let alone locate, what I was supposed to be looking for.

Somehow, with Geoff and the inspector's help, I managed to gather a few things together and put them into a bag. Geoff took it. We stood in the kitchen knowing that our time was almost up.

'Have you any money?' Mr Smith asked. My husband pulled a five pound note from his pocket and offered it to me saying, 'You'd better have this.'

'No, you keep it,' I said. 'You'll need it for cigarettes and things.'

He put the money back into his pocket.

The inspector said, 'You'd better say goodbye now.' He went into the hall and stood with his back to us. Geoff and I clung to one another.

Since then I have often tried to imagine my husband's feelings at that moment. Mine were of total despair and aloneness.

We let one another go and walked down the hall with the inspector and three of his men. One of them opened the front door and we all walked out and then along the drive.

At the gate I blurted out, 'What happens now?'

Mr Smith said, 'We'll let your husband ring you later today.'

My husband, accompanied by the policemen, was starting to move away from me and I cried out in sudden anguish, 'Don't leave me, Geoff!' He gave me a last despairing look and a squeeze of the hand, before lowering himself into the back seat of the police car.

As it moved off, I waved, seeing his face framed in the rear window as he kept it turned towards me till the last possible moment.

When he was out of sight, I stood on the pavement, suffering the first raw pangs of separation. The thing I had dreaded had happened. I could no longer pretend that it had all been a nightmare.

I turned and started to walk back to the house. The two policemen who had been searching the garage came out to meet me, followed by the policewoman.

One of the men said, 'We'll be taking the car away now.'

'Do!' I said, feelingly.

'Now what about you?' the man went on. 'You mustn't be on your own.'

'I'll stay with you,' answered the policewoman. I shook my head.

'It's kind of you, but I don't want anyone. Really.'

'Is there someone you can ring?' the man asked.

'Yes, my parents. They're not far away.'

'All right, as long as you promise to ring them.'

'I will,' I said. The two men got into our car and drove away.

The woman lingered, looking at me with concern.

'I think I should come in and stay with you for a bit,' she said.

'No, please go,' I said urgently.

'Are you sure you're all right?'

'Yes, I'll ring my parents,' I told her.

'Well, here's my phone number, just in case. Ring me any time.' She handed me a card.

'Thank you,' I said, taking it, and then, with a sense of relief, watched her turn and walk towards the gate. The police had been necessary. They had even been kind. But, as well as being strangers, they had been instrumental in parting Geoff and myself. What I needed now, urgently, was someone loved and familiar.

I went into the house, closing the front door behind me, then made for the lounge. With shaking hands, I picked up the phone and dialled my parents' number.

'Dad, come quick – something awful's happened,' I blurted out.

'What's the matter?' was his instant reaction.

'Geoff's gone,' I answered. 'Just come as soon as you can.'

He drove round, under the impression, as I later discovered, that I must have finally made up my mind to leave Geoff or he me.

Arriving at our house, he let himself in and hurried to the kitchen. At the sight of him, I broke into hysterical weeping. He stood near me, holding my shoulders. After a while, I heard him exclaim, 'We'd better close the front door. Everyone will have heard you.' Beyond caring, I went on screaming, crying and sobbing. He closed the front door, then continued to hold and comfort me as best he could.

When the worst was over, I braced myself and said to him, 'You'd better sit down.' He did so. Then I told him of Geoff's arrest in connection with sexual offences.

Remaining outwardly calm, he listened. Then, utterly at a loss, he said, 'We'd better go and tell Mother. She was just cooking the lunch when I left.'

'I couldn't eat a thing,' I protested.

'No, but you can't stay here on your own,' he replied.

He steadied and supported me as I walked with him to the car. I collapsed into the passenger seat and sat there, feeling dazed and exhausted, as we drove along.

Dad was silent for a few moments. Then he said, quietly, 'Well, Rhona, you're on your own again. It's the story of your life, isn't it? You're going to have to sort things out your way.'

'You're right,' I agreed wearily. It was an opinion I was to revise in the near future.

Mum had been waiting anxiously for us to arrive. When we did she gave me a big hug, then, taking my arm, led me into the sitting room and made me sit down. A moment later, dad handed me a sherry. I raised the glass unsteadily to my mouth and took a sip.

'Now what's all this about?' my mother asked.

I told her what I had told dad. The shock of this revelation must have been colossal but my parents managed to keep their own feelings under control and be a strength and comfort to me.

I stayed at the house for a while, trying to pull myself together enough to go home and face the boys.

What was I going to say? I was far too confused to be able to work anything out. I would simply have to muddle through somehow.

Dad drove me home and then went back to mum.

Craig arrived first and came into the kitchen. I greeted him, then told him, 'I'm afraid Geoff's had to go away on business to do with the wine company and I don't know when he'll be back.' My youngest son accepted that, but looked sad.

I was in the lounge when Mark and Stephen arrived home. One look at my face must have told them that I'd been crying.

'I've got something important to tell you,' I said. 'You'd better come in and sit down.' They did so. For a moment I couldn't speak.

'Is it about business?' Mark asked.

I shook my head, then blurted out, 'Geoff's been taken away to prison.'

The room went very quiet. Then, playing for time, I asked, 'Can you imagine what it might be for?'

Mark was to tell me later that spying had come into his mind but he'd quickly dismissed that as being too fantastic. Instead he guessed, 'Drugs? Burglary?'

'No,' I answered. Then, knowing there was no putting it

off any longer, I said, in anguish, 'It's to do with assaults on girls.'

There was a stunned silence from the boys.

'I don't want Craig to know just yet,' I went on. 'He thinks Geoff is away on business.'

I started to cry and the boys tactfully withdrew. There was more to be said but not just then. I couldn't manage it and they probably wanted to be left alone for a while.

Soon afterwards the phone rang. I went to answer it. It was Geoff. The sound of his voice had me crying again. He sounded very emotional, too.

'Where are you? What are they doing to you?' I asked.

'I'm in Hereford, in one of the police cells. They're going to keep me here for questioning – I don't know for how long.'

'Where will you go next?'

'Gloucester Prison. They're going to charge me tomorrow.'

I flinched, then asked, 'What's it like? How are they treating you?'

'It's not too bad, and I'm all right,' he replied.

'Can I come and see you?'

'Yes, on Saturday. They said I could ring you again or you could contact me.'

There was a fraught silence. Then he said, unnecessarily, 'I feel dreadful.'

'So do I,' I answered. 'But we've just got to get through this somehow.'

'Yes,' he said. 'I'm sure it will be for the best in the long run.'

'I'd better go and get the tea ready for the boys,' I said, feeling that the strain was getting too much for both of us.

'All right. I'll ring you tomorrow. Goodbye.'

'Goodbye, Geoff.'

I put the phone down and started sobbing. After a while, I dried my eyes and tried to face up to what lay ahead. There were the boys to think of and work to be done. The evening had to be managed, somehow.

In the course of it, a surprisingly clear thought came to me:

I must write all this down. Otherwise it will seem too fantastic and unreal to be believed by me or anyone. But it took me several days to implement this idea, and a huge effort of will to keep writing in the journal over the next weeks and months.

The next day Geoff was charged with a sexual offence and then taken to Hereford Magistrates' Court to be remanded. I existed in a stupefied state which did not protect me from the agony of seeing the 'story' in the local paper that evening or lessen the heartache I felt for the girls and their families and for my own children.

I kept the paper from Craig, but felt that the time had come to tell him the truth as gently as possible, lest he should learn of it in some other way.

'I'm afraid Geoff's not away on business,' I told him. 'He's done something bad and has had to go to prison. But he didn't mean to be bad. He's sick in his mind and they're going to make him better.'

Craig was shocked and tearful. I did my best to comfort him, as well as Mark and Stephen, who could not be protected from the newspapers. My two older sons, however, didn't want to talk about the situation with me. Like me, they were, I think, too stunned and dazed to do much more than simply get through the day.

Then Jane rang up. She and I had got to know one another in our teens when we'd both attended the same church. We'd become friends at that time and had continued to meet one another spasmodically – sometimes by arrangement, at other times accidentally. Jane had been a great help to me at the time of my divorce from Peter. Then I'd married Geoff and after that we'd only met occasionally. Now, having seen the papers, she was ringing to offer help and friendship.

'It's been a terrible, terrible shock,' I told her. 'And things could get worse. I can't talk about it on the phone. Can I come and see you?'

'Yes of course,' she replied, and we arranged to meet in the following week.

The burden of Geoff's second confession was weighing

very heavily on me. On Friday, unable to bear it alone any longer, I confided in my mother.

The impact of this new revelation was devastating for her. I understood her feelings only too well. Now there were two of us reeling with overwhelming shock and pain.

In this state, I faced the prospect of my first visit to Geoff since his arrest.

8

The visit

It was Bank Holiday Saturday – a day of sun and showers. Three days had passed since Geoff had been taken away and I was standing in the foyer of Hereford Police Station. My parents had driven me there and were close by. Before being admitted to this big modern building, we had checked that our car was in the police car park. Seeing it again had proved an almost unbearable experience for me. *As soon as I get it back, I'll sell it and get a different one*, I'd promised myself.

Now I approached the woman sitting behind the counter and said, 'I've come to see Mr Prime.'

'And you are –?' she enquired.

'Mrs Prime, his wife,' I supplied. 'And these are my parents who want to visit for a few moments, too.'

'Please take a seat while I find out where he is,' she said. We went and sat on a bench. I was only vaguely aware of my surroundings and of people coming and going. After a time, in an effort to relax, I started to look around.

Headlines screamed at me from wall posters: Wanted for murder. Wanted for armed robbery. Underneath were blown-up photographs or identikit pictures of the people who had committed these appalling crimes and were still at large.

I felt crushed. Having to be in a place like this brought home to me afresh the horror of our situation.

The woman came back and said, 'I'll take you through,' and raised a flap in the counter. We walked through the gap and followed her down a short corridor.

Approaching us was a familiar figure – that of Detective Chief Inspector Smith.

'Hullo, Mrs Prime. How are you?' he said, using the conventional and – in the circumstances – silly words to tide us over an awkward moment.

'Not too bad,' I lied in the same vein. He greeted my parents and then I asked, 'How's Geoff?'

'Fair,' he replied. 'I'll just have to check what you've brought him.'

I showed him books, newspapers and cigarettes. He examined them quickly before handing them back with a smile and the invitation, 'Come this way.'

We went deeper into the building. The inspector opened a door. My heart thumping painfully, I stepped into the room. It was small and windowless – the light coming from an overhead bulb. Geoff was seated on a chair. Seeing me, he stood up and came towards me.

'I'll leave you to it,' the inspector said, going out and leaving the door slightly ajar behind him. My husband and I kissed one another, crying a little. Then he and my parents spoke to each other for the first time since the arrest. It was a difficult moment for everyone. After a short exchange dad left, to be followed, a few moments later, by mum, when she'd handed Geoff a letter and Bible and promised to be back for me in an hour.

Left alone, we sat down with the table between us. The only other furniture was a wall bench.

'Is this your room?' I asked, noticing how drawn he looked.

'No, this is a visiting room. My cell's further along that way,' he said, indicating the general direction.

'What's it like?'

'Pretty basic, but I do have my own toilet. My bed is a bench with a mattress on it and there's a window high up in the wall. If I want to have a shower, I have to ask and then wait for someone to unlock the doors and take me there and back.'

'What are the police like?'

'Doing their best. They bring me meals and are quite pleasant. Usually people are only kept here overnight, but they won't be able to get me in anywhere else until after the Bank Holiday.'

He asked me how I was coping. I forced myself to deal with practical matters. What should I do about our credit cards? What bills would be coming in and how would I pay?

We talked, too, of the boys and my parents.

Our every word is being overheard! was the thought that kept coming to me. The sheer indignity was hard to bear. Were there to be no private conversations between us, I wondered desperately. How would we be able to cope? Geoff would find this lack of privacy even harder to bear than I.

Our hour was nearly up. The inspector came in carrying a thick pile of papers and saying, 'I need to have a chat with you.' He sat down on the bench and placed the papers on the table.

'When will Geoff be going to Gloucester?' I asked.

'I don't know yet, but it'll be soon, because we haven't the facilities for keeping people in the police station. But he'll have to come back here each week to be remanded, until he is committed for trial.'

'When will that be?'

'I can't say,' he answered. 'There's a great deal of work to be done.' He indicated the papers and continued, 'We have to check that no other offences have to be taken into account, and that involves following up the phone numbers and addresses on the index cards.'

My mind reeled. It was a case of changing the subject or going under completely.

'How will I know when he's moved?' I asked.

'We'll let you know,' he promised, then added, 'Tell you what – as it's Bank Holiday, you can have another visit on Monday, if you like.'

'Thank you. I'd love to come if I can,' I said.

Time was up. After a painful, emotional parting from Geoff, I was escorted back to the foyer.

'When will I get the car back?' I asked.

'In about a fortnight's time,' said the inspector. 'I'm afraid it's got a bald tyre, so that will have to be seen to when you get it back.'

One more thing! I thought despondently.

I left the police station and went across to my parents' car. They were sitting inside it, waiting. One look at my face, and mum suggested tea.

It was as we were walking towards the town, hoping to find a café, that we saw the hoardings. There in huge letters we read, 'Sex attacker wanted,' followed by a description of the man they were looking for.

For a few seconds the words conjured up a horrific figure but one that was unreal and remote.

Then realisation hit me like a thunderbolt: *They're talking about the person to whom I've just been speaking – the man with whom I've been sharing my life for the past five years – my husband – Geoff.*

For the first time in my life, confronted by such words, I could not merely shudder and pass by, secure in the knowledge that this was someone else's nightmare. This time I was involved. So, therefore, were my parents.

I could see the pain and shock in their eyes as we turned and made for the nearest café. There, we ordered tea. I nearly choked on mine. Then came the ordeal of the walk back to the car, past the poster – which shouldn't still have been there, adding unnecessarily to our sufferings, and which was dangerously misleading since Geoff's problem was rooted in voyeurism and he had not sexually assaulted the girls.

For the rest of the day I functioned, but only just. Craig was sad and tearful and Mark and Stephen seemed bemused and depressed, still not wanting to talk about the situation with me. I worried about all three of them – and about Geoff.

I kept thinking about the way he had been during the visit: haggard and upset, naturally, but not nearly as downcast as he could have been, and certainly not as defeated and despondent as he'd been in the weeks before his arrest.

Why? I asked myself. The answer had to be that now, at last, he saw a glimmer of hope ahead. He would take his punishment, receive the help he needed and come out a free man, ready to lead a new life.

Would it really be that simple? What about the spying business? Was it real or was it fantasy? Either way, what was I going to do about it?

After a bad night, I woke early.

It was Sunday. In desperation, clutching at straws, I thought, *I'll go to church. Perhaps someone there will show me what to do or help me.*

9

The wallet

The church was a big old building – rather gloomy inside. I took my seat along with the other worshippers and tried to concentrate.

My parents being Christians, I'd been brought up to attend church, and once during my teens I'd really felt committed to Jesus Christ for a time. But an early marriage, three children, constant moves and financial and other problems had crowded out my faith. From time to time, particularly when desperate, I'd gone back to church, hoping for help and strength. In some churches I'd received it, in others I hadn't. Whenever I'd found genuine, caring people, I would worship with them for a while, but then I'd move away or get caught up in events or else my situation would improve and I'd feel capable of managing my own affairs again.

Once, at a very low ebb after the divorce, I had been particularly touched by the sincerity and love of a group of Christians with whom I'd come into contact. At one of their gatherings a man had told me that something bad would happen in my life and that I would turn back to God. He had also said that he could see that I would have to go through a long, dark tunnel, but that there would be light at the end of it. I hadn't been too sure about the tunnel but certainly something bad *had* happened in my life, namely the divorce, and I *had*, I felt, come back to God.

At about the same time, but in a different place and by a different minister, my mother had been given much the same warning and hope.

Not long afterwards I'd met Geoff and made up my mind that he was God's provision for me and the boys. Then, as before, the onrush of events had absorbed me. I'd still gone to church, but only occasionally and what I'd heard and seen there hadn't seemed relevant to my life. Geoff, a nominal Catholic, had long since given up church attendance.

Now, five years after our marriage and truly desperate this time, I was in church again. But it wasn't until the sermon that my attention was fully caught and held. The minister was speaking on the last verse of Romans chapter twelve. I was struck by the words: 'Do not be overcome by evil; but overcome evil with good.'

This is for me, I thought. God was speaking to me, I felt; telling me to go on loving and helping Geoff. I was moved and began to weep.

After the service I was asked whether I would like to see the minister. When I said yes, I was taken to a side room to wait until he had said goodbye to his congregation. A few moments later, he came into the room and I told him, rather incoherently, that I wanted to speak to him about a private matter.

'Yes of course,' he said. Very brokenly, I began to pour out my heart to him about our situation and my own total confusion. As I spoke, I became aware of a reaction of shock and horror in him. I stopped speaking and after a stunned silence he said, 'Perhaps it's not as bad as you think. Your husband could, as you suggest, be fantasising about the spying.'

'But what do you think I should do?'

'All I can say at the moment is that I feel you may need a solicitor and I suggest that it would be good to have a Christian one; if you like I'll make some enquiries about one for you.'

I felt terribly let down.

'I would like to share all this with my wife, if you don't mind,' he continued.

'No – that'll be all right,' I said dispiritedly.

'I'll be in touch with you during the week, but we'll pray now,' he said.

His prayer left me feeling even more deflated. He sounded like a man out of his depth. Being in the same state myself, this was little help to me.

I went home still racked with indecision and, after a grim day, passed a sleepless night.

The next day, Bank Holiday Monday, I went to see Geoff again. It was another strained, emotional, exhausting visit.

'I can't cope with this any longer – we're going to have to speak to your father about it,' mum said, when I next saw her. I agreed, and we broke the news to dad. He, though equally shattered, said that he felt I should go to the authorities and tell them what Geoff had told me. The mere thought of doing that was torture.

On Tuesday Geoff was transferred to Gloucester Prison and I went about in a daze of misery, scarcely knowing what I was doing. The following day I went to see him.

I'd hardly ever seen, let alone visited, a prison before. Yet here I was – walking towards the thick, black, wooden doors of Gloucester Prison, knowing that my husband was locked up somewhere inside the building.

My parents, always ready to help in practical ways, had driven me over and would be returning for me afterwards. I was aware of their suffering and their struggle to come to terms with what had happened to their daughter.

Someone banged the huge metal knocker and a moment later the door was opened and a guard appeared. I noticed the large bunch of keys attached to his belt. He asked each of us who we were and our business, before admitting us, then locking up behind us.

Keys jangling as he walked, he led us up stone steps and along stone passages. In one corridor, on the left, I noticed some wooden partitions partly enclosing bench-seats below grilled windows. I had seen prisoners and their families talking to one another through such grills on television and in films but seeing the real thing brought home to me the degradation and frustration involved.

Would I have to communicate with Geoff like that, I wondered despairingly.

But I was led past the partitions and along more corridors until, after much unlocking and relocking of doors, we reached the waiting room.

I wanted to turn and run from the noisy, smoke-filled place, but instead I found a chair and sat down.

Grubby, scruffily-dressed children were darting about amongst prams, push-chairs and waiting people. Some people sat on chairs, others were perched on tables. Most talked loudly amongst themselves – breaking off now and again to yell at the children. A few, like myself, sat alone and silent. For the most part, we must have looked a poor, inadequate bunch – whether typical of local prison visitors or not I didn't know. In some faces I saw hopelessness, in others defiant hardness.

Every now and then an officer would enter and call out, 'Visitors for Bloggs, (or whoever)' – and someone, or an assorted group, would move towards the gate which would be duly unlocked for them and afterwards relocked.

'Visitors for Prime!'

It was my turn at last. I stood up and self-consciously made for the gate. Beyond it lay a courtyard. After the stuffiness of the waiting room, the fresh air smelt good and a small flower bed added a touch of colour to the otherwise drab surroundings. The officer led me across the courtyard, past some of his colleagues and a few prisoners, towards a wooden hut.

On entering it, my heart sank. Here was another crowded, noisy room. I stood at a desk and told the officer behind it my name, address and the person I had come to visit. He wrote these particulars into a large book, then asked me to show him what I had brought.

I handed over toothpaste, cigarettes, magazines and newspapers.

'You can take the cigarettes in,' he told me. 'And the other things will be checked and delivered later.' Then, stretching out an arm to point, he said, 'Your husband's over there.'

I followed the direction he had indicated, threading my way past groups of people sitting on wooden chairs round blue formica-topped tables.

Then I saw Geoff, coming to meet me. We hugged one another in a constrained manner, then sat down at one of the tables. I gave him the cigarettes and he lit one. His face looked pale and tense.

'How is it?' I asked.

'Bad,' he said. 'No peace at all. There are two others in my cell. They play cards all the time and have the wireless blaring out pop music all day.'

'What was the journey like?'

'Rather grim. They brought me here in a police van. How are you?'

'Not too bad. The doctor signed me off work.'

'And the boys?'

'Stephen and Mark aren't saying much. Craig obviously misses you.'

There was so much to sort out and so little time. Among other mundane questions I asked, 'Where's our AA card?' adding, 'I want to pick up the handbook as soon as possible.'

'It'll be in my wallet – in the desk,' he said.

There were other practical matters to discuss.

'Time up for Prime,' a guard called and our fifteen minutes was over. In such a short time we hadn't even begun to adjust to the noisy, unnatural atmosphere, let alone say anything of real importance to one another.

Mum and dad drove me home and came indoors with me. I went up to our bedroom and opened the desk. Geoff's wallet was lying there. I picked it up and opened it. Inside were various cards and papers. I quickly found what I was looking for – our AA membership card.

Then my attention was drawn to something else. It was a tiny plastic sachet, and there was another one like it. I opened one of them and took out what was inside. It was a minute pad – its pages covered with numbers.

As I stood and stared at them, the word *microfilm* flashed into my mind and I felt the stab of fear. I called my parents up and saw their disturbed expressions as they looked at the sachets.

'It seems as though our worst fears are confirmed,' my father said.

'What are you going to do, Rhona?' mum asked gently. In deep agitation I replied, 'I don't know. I've got to think about it.'

My father went downstairs and made tea. We followed and took a cup each. I don't think I drank mine. My parents were concerned for me, but obviously they had to leave me to make my own decision.

Round and round went my thoughts as I struggled through the rest of the day and the night that followed it.

What was I to do? Here was what looked like incriminating evidence. Why had Geoff left it around? Why hadn't the police find it and taken it away? There were no answers and the onus now lay on me.

Where should my loyalties lie? With my husband, who I felt sure had acted out of a desire to bring about a fairer, juster world, albeit by terribly wrong means? With my country which – for all its faults – I loved? If I were to go to the authorities, those whom I loved would suffer even more than they had already. If I were to remain silent, how would I be able to live with my conscience? Thanks to the Christian upbringing which my parents had given me, I had been taught to value truth. By inclination, too, I preferred to have everything out in the open and faced honestly. But that would involve betraying my husband . . .

10

Indecision

The next day the minister came to see me. He had telephoned once or twice to assure me of his prayers and give me the name of a Christian solicitor. Now, sitting in my lounge, he asked, 'How are you, Rhona?'

Biting back a waspish *How do you think I am?* I told him a little about what had been happening.

'My wife and I think you should divorce this man,' he said.

I was taken aback. This wasn't the advice I had expected from a minister – particularly in view of his sermon the previous Sunday. We talked for a while and then he went, promising to pray for me but leaving me more confused than ever.

On Friday, May 7th, Geoff was charged with two other sexual offences and again taken to Hereford Magistrates' Court to be remanded – this latter being a procedure which was to take place every Friday until his committal for trial.

It was a relief to meet Jane and share some of my desperation and confusion with this long-standing, level-headed friend. There was no doubt in her mind as to what I should do about my suspicions concerning Geoff's espionage, but I said, 'I need more time to think about that,' adding, 'It's easy for you to tell me to go to the authorities – but how would you like it if it was your husband you were going to inform on?'

She seemed to see the point. Later in the conversation she asked, 'What if Geoff's contacts try to get in touch with you?'

'Thanks a lot!' I responded with a rueful laugh and a shudder.

'I don't want to worry you,' she said, then reminded me of a recent presumed-Russian reprisal in London. Having scared one another silly, we parted, promising to keep in regular touch and to pray for one another's protection.

The idea that the foreign gentleman or one of his associates would contact me started to prey on my mind. Particularly when I was on my own and at night, the ringing of the telephone would have me imagining all sorts of sinister possibilities.

On Sunday, without much enthusiasm, I attended church again. People were polite but didn't really 'want to know', I felt. Perhaps I was over-sensitive and therefore misjudged them.

'I'm praying for you,' the minister told me.

I thought, *The next time anyone says that to me, I'll scream!* I appreciated the fact that people were telling God about my needs, but wasn't he asking any of them, or didn't any of them care enough, to help meet those needs? I was desperate just then for comfort, support and practical help.

I received a letter from Geoff giving me his prison number and telling me to write it on any envelope addressed to him. I stared in horror at the digits. Hearing him referred to as 'Prime' was bad enough. Now, it seemed, he was a cypher.

On the encouraging side, two new people began to take an interest in Geoff and started writing to him, praying for him and occasionally visiting him. One was an Anglican vicar named Adrian Hirst who had been visiting another prisoner at Gloucester – someone whom Geoff had got to know. When that prisoner left, it was arranged, through mutual agreement, that the minister should visit Geoff instead. The other person was a Christian counsellor and a retired teacher whom I had met through a teacher friend of mine. Both these men were to become very supportive to us as a family.

Meanwhile, feeling utterly insecure and buffeted by my own fluctuating feelings and confused thoughts, I was in an excruciating dilemma.

What was I to do about Geoff? With my own mind and heart in a state of painful turmoil, I had to look elsewhere for answers and found myself swept to and fro by the attitudes and opinions of others. Gradually, and with great reluctance, I began to feel that those whom I sensed wanted me to divorce my husband and those who actually advised me to do so, couldn't all be wrong.

And then there were the sachets and what Geoff had told me about his spying activities. What was I to do about all that? The agonising answer that was emerging, and the only course of action that I could square with my conscience, was that I should go to the authorities – albeit hoping with all my heart that things would not be as serious as they seemed.

Reaching these tentative decisions brought no relief. The future filled me with acute alarm. More immediately, I was overcome with dread at the thought of having to tell Geoff the conclusions I had reached. But I knew this was what I had to do.

The next visiting day arrived and as usual I had a kind chauffeur to drive me to and from the prison. On this occasion, Jane came with me too, to lend support both before and after the visit. I left her sitting in the car with the driver while I went inside.

After the usual procedures I was escorted to the same big noisy room.

Geoff's appearance proved an unexpected shock. A prison haircut and uniform had transformed him overnight from an ordinary person into someone who looked like a criminal. I tried not to stare in dismay at his blue-and-white striped shirt and grey trousers, but inside I felt shaken.

Geoff was very distressed and I could not bring myself to tell him what I had come to say. Instead, I mentioned my fears about his Soviet contacts. These, he assured me, were groundless. We tried to talk of other things, but the atmosphere was very strained. Near the end of our fifteen minutes I blurted out, 'Geoff, I can't live with this any more. I'm going to have to tell the authorities about it.'

He understood my reference immediately and looked acutely disturbed. Then in tones of weary despair, he said, 'If you can put me away for life, Rhona, go and do it.'

I was completely winded. It wouldn't have surprised me if he'd said, 'Don't do it,' though what I'd hoped to hear him say was, 'Don't worry – it's not serious.' But never, even in my worst moments, had I imagined such a response.

In great distress but trying to hide it, I hurriedly said goodbye and left.

Not until we were on our own in the back garden at home was I able to talk freely to Jane about the visit. She looked perturbed, and said, 'Be careful, Rhona. You know how impulsive you are.'

Though not yet convinced about the action I should take, I decided to speak to the Christian solicitor whose name I had been given.

My father went with me to my first appointment with him, but I found Mr Bowden easy to talk to – a quiet, shy, kind person, I thought. I told him I was considering the possibility of separation or divorce and gave him the relevant facts about the arrest. He listened attentively, then advised me about possible procedures. I replied that I was still not sure about what to do and made an appointment to see him again the following day, which was Friday.

Meantime, as well as agonising about whether to go ahead with separation or divorce, I had to decide whether to tell Mr Bowden about Geoff's possible involvement in spying.

My husband's words kept ringing ominously in my ears. Previously I'd coped with the idea of going to the authorities by telling myself either that Geoff had imagined himself to be a spy or that he had been an unimportant one. But his words seemed to indicate that his espionage activities had been both real and serious. So going to the authorities would mean that he'd be away for far longer than the few years I'd been hopefully envisaging. It was a shattering thought. Yet if his spying was of this order, wasn't it all the more important that I should speak out? Reluctantly, I concluded that it was.

I arrived at Mr Bowden's office the next day, knowing what I had to do but hating the apparent treachery to my husband. With shaking hands, I took Geoff's wallet from my bag and passed it over to the solicitor, telling him what I had found inside and what I feared. He looked at the sachets and the rest of the contents, then said quietly, 'The choice is yours. But this looks serious, so for everyone's sake it would be advisable to hand these things over.'

'I'm afraid so,' I said miserably.

'How would you like to go about it? Who would you like me to contact?'

'Detective Chief Inspector Smith of Hereford Police Force,' I said. I had always found him helpful and had had more to do with him than with anyone else among the police.

Mr Bowden rang Hereford Police Station and a moment later I heard him say, 'This is Mr Bowden acting on behalf of Mrs Prime of Pittville Crescent Lane, Cheltenham. She has something she wishes to discuss with you as soon as possible.'

After a pause, putting a hand over the mouthpiece, he queried, 'Would Monday, twelve o'clock, at your house be all right?'

'Couldn't it be sooner?' I asked, hating the thought of such a heavy cloud hanging over me. Mr Bowden made the request but was soon shaking his head, so I agreed to Monday and he rang off. Suddenly panic-stricken I said, 'What have I done?' Mr Bowden responded gently, 'Why don't you think and pray about it over the weekend and I'll do the same and give you a ring on Monday to see how you feel.'

'All right,' I agreed, without enthusiasm.

'Perhaps we should draft a statement now,' he continued, 'so that I could go through it with you on Monday before the police arrive.'

Home again after that traumatic exercise I went about my duties feeling like a zombie and racked with indecision and resentment.

Why was all this happening to me? What had I done to deserve so much? How could I, a mere human being, cope with it? My anger, directed first against the God in whom I vaguely believed, was switched to Geoff. How could he have done what he did, causing me and those whom I loved so much suffering? The next moment, remembering my husband's good qualities, I was appalled at what I had done and was contemplating.

Saturday crawled by and then Sunday. Monday was now looming very close. If only someone would help me or show me what to do!

On Sunday night, something unexpected happened.

11

Breaking point

Leaving the hall light on as usual in my highly nervous state, I went into the bedroom and undressed. Then, also as usual, I peered fearfully under the bed before getting into it.

There was something there. Why on earth hadn't I seen it before? With a fast-beating heart, I reached under and pulled it out.

It was an ordinary brown paper carrier bag with a well known brand name printed on it. I straightened up, bag in hand, and tipped the contents on to the bed. Envelopes came spilling out. I looked them over. They were all addressed to East Berlin.

I opened one, pulled out the paper inside and unfolded it. It was a typed letter, which I started to read.

'I've got a new car. How is yours? The family is fine. The children are growing fast. The garden is keeping me busy . . .'

I didn't have to read much more in the same vein before the truth sank in. These letters were in code.

For the second time I had been the unwitting finder of things which seemed to implicate Geoff in espionage.

Why me? I thought, despairingly. And what had possessed Geoff to leave all this lying around? And what was I supposed to do with it?

Panic-stricken ideas flashed through my mind. Should I throw the letters in Pittville Lake or burn them? *No*, I decided, my mind clearing. I had been agonising over what to do and finding the bag just then had to be confirmation to go ahead and speak to the authorities. And when I did that, I'd have to tell the *whole* truth, and that would involve handing in the letters with the wallet.

The decision finally made, I returned the letters to the bag and got into bed. It was a long, dark night.

In the morning, I dragged myself out of bed and got the boys breakfasted and off to school. Then I telephoned my parents, and dad promised to be round before the police arrived.

Mr Bowden rang and asked how I felt about things.

I answered woodenly, 'I'll go ahead as planned.'

At about half-past eleven Mr Bowden arrived, bringing the wallet which he had kept in his safe over the weekend. He showed me the statement. It said that Geoff had confessed to me that he'd been a spy, that a few days after leaving GCHQ he'd set off with the intention of going to Helsinki, and that I had found two small polythene sachets in his wallet containing what I thought was microfilm.

Feeling wretched, I signed the paper, then forced myself to say, 'Last night I found something strange. I'll show you.'

I went upstairs, returning a moment later with one of the letters from the carrier bag.

'That's one of many,' I said, handing it to him. He took and read it.

'What are you going to do about it?' he asked, quietly.

'I'll have to hand it over with all the others and the wallet,' I said, unhappily. 'I haven't any choice really, have I?'

The doorbell rang and someone walked in – my father's usual way of announcing himself. I was glad that he'd be with me. When he came in we brought him up to date. I returned the letter to the carrier bag while waiting tensely for the doorbell to ring again. At midday it did, setting my heart thumping wildly. On the doorstep stood Detective Chief Inspector Smith and a colleague – both in plain clothes. We went into the lounge and sat down – the two men and I on the sofa, and dad and Mr Bowden on easy chairs.

After the usual polite, hollow banalities, the chief inspector said, 'Well, Rhona, what is it you want to tell us?'

I was suddenly speechless and my eyes filled with tears. Mr Bowden handed over the statement. The two men read it in silence. I passed over the wallet. They looked at all its contents and noted them down.

'There's something else,' I gulped, making a quick exit. Feeling dazed and wretched, I fetched the carrier bag and brought it down to the lounge. Mr Smith took it from me. Once again he and his colleagues examined the contents, then listed them.

'Thank you, Rhona,' Mr Smith said, looking at me with a grave expression. 'We're going to have to take all this away and investigate it further. And I'm afraid we'll need to have your husband's passport too.'

I found it and handed it over, wondering how much more of this torture I could stand.

'Before we go,' Mr Smith said, 'is there anything else you want to tell us?'

I made a desperate effort to address my confused mind to this question and managed to remember something.

'I've a ten pound note left from some money Geoff gave me and I think it may be dirty money, but I really need it – so must you take it as well?' I said.

'I'm afraid so,' he answered. 'But you'll get it back later.'

I took the note from my handbag and gave it to him, then signed for what they were taking away: the money, the twenty-six envelopes, the passport, the two sachets and a slip of paper containing instructions of some sort which had also been in the wallet.

'We'll have to go now,' Mr Smith said. In the hall, on our way to the door, he added kindly, 'Try not to worry too much. Some people do fantasise that they're James Bond or whoever. They're the ones who are more likely to leave evidence lying around because often they seem to get a kick out of seeing it there.'

'I really hope that's all there is to it,' I said, adding, 'And please, just for the moment, don't tell Geoff about this.'

'We won't,' Mr Smith assured me.

The police and Mr Bowden left and dad drove me to

mum's for lunch. Food was the last thing on my mind but getting away from a house now so full of anguished memories gave me a 'breather'.

My parents tried to reassure me that I had done the right thing, which I knew, but I still felt torn apart.

The dark shadow of my coming visit to Geoff hung over me on Tuesday and then came the day itself, Wednesday. Again I was driving to the prison, trying to prepare myself to cope with the emotional strain of the visit and to say what needed to be said.

In acute apprehension, I entered the visiting room and made my way over to Geoff. Inhibited by the unnatural situation, we greeted one another and sat down to talk. As I looked into his familiar face and listened to him, the confusion in my mind seemed to resolve itself. I saw Geoff, the man, as he truly was or could be. He had done terrible things and deserved to be punished – certainly. But he was not the utterly ruthless, evil, inhuman figure that it was almost possible to believe him to be, through listening to others or simply thinking about what he had done. He was a human being, with good as well as bad qualities, and deep psychological problems. I, if no one else, knew that. What's more, he was my husband, and I was far too deeply involved with him and all that he was enduring and would have to endure, to walk away. I now knew that I couldn't do that, even if I'd wanted to – which I didn't.

What we talked about I'm not sure. Perhaps it was on this visit that I told him how pleased I'd been to hear that he'd helped and befriended another prisoner, but he brushed the praise aside.

'It was nothing. Don't make so much of it. Anyone would have done the same,' he said.

I returned home, without having found the courage to tell Geoff what I had done, but knowing that my indecision concerning the other matter was over. I cared about my husband, was involved and would continue to be involved with his life.

Wanting to let Mr Bowden know of my decision, I rang for

an appointment and was given one for Friday. On Thursday morning I went to see and talk to mum. She realised that the trauma of indecision and decision making had left me close to cracking up, and promptly offered to pay for Craig and myself to have a week's break at half-term, starting the following day. Stephen and Mark were already going to be away at their grandparents' in Bideford. I accepted her kindness gratefully, and arrangements were made with a guest-house in Dartmouth.

That evening, mum and I were due to go to a meal and meeting arranged by the Full Gospel Businessmen's Fellowship International – FGBMFI for short. When she'd invited me to this event I'd accepted. Though not feeling particularly well-disposed to Christians at the time, I'd jumped at the chance of a few hours' relief or diversion from my problems. Besides, a long while before, I'd been to one or two meetings arranged by this organisation and recalled that they'd been pleasantly different from the usual type of church gathering.

My mother and I, and others going to the meeting, met at a smart hotel in Cheltenham. Everyone seemed friendly and the three-course meal was excellent. Then the meeting began – with people singing lively songs. Afterwards a man stood up to speak. Within seconds he had me hanging on every word. This was no sermon but a personal story.

He told us how he had gone his own way in life and made a mess of things.

That's me, I thought.

At rock bottom, he had finally turned to God asking for forgiveness and had received a new, satisfying, worthwhile life with Jesus Christ in complete charge.

'If there are any here who want to commit their lives to Jesus Christ but are not quite sure how to do it,' he said, 'would you please come to the front and there will be people here to help you.'

Suddenly I knew this was what I wanted to do. Crying, my heart pounding, I made my way forward and stood at a long table.

12

Lifeline

A man came to stand on the other side of the table opposite me.

'My name is Paul Snow,' he said, giving me a friendly smile. There was no way I could return it, but after swallowing a few times, I managed to reply, 'And I'm Rhona Prime.'

Paul Snow asked gently, 'Are you a Christian? Do you know God?'

'I was brought up as a Christian and was quite committed for a short time in my teens,' I said. 'But I feel I need to recommit my life to God.'

He held my hands across the table and prayed, asking God to forgive me and come into my life. I added a heartfelt 'Amen'.

'Everything in my life's such a mess,' I said dismally, and went on to speak of our situation. I could sense his deep sympathy but after a while, overcome by anguish, I broke down and cried – tears of agony, not relief. When I had become calmer, he said, 'Would you like to spend more time on this with my wife and me?'

I nodded, adding, 'This is too short – too public.'

'I'll ring you next week,' he said.

'I'm going away for a while,' I told him. 'Shall I get in touch with you when I get back?'

'Please do, but we'll pray now too.'

He gripped my hands and started praying. Distraught though I was, I recognised at once that this was a new kind of prayer. Paul Snow was telling God what I had just told him, as though he were talking to someone standing close by: someone whom he knew very well and who, he felt confident, cared and would actually do something about my situation.

As he prayed, something began to change, as I experienced, deep inside me, the first faint glow of peace. With all my heart I said 'Amen' at the end.

Afterwards he asked, 'Do you attend church?'

'I've gone to various churches over the years,' I said. 'But I don't know where to go at the moment.'

'Why not try Elim?' he suggested. I had noticed the attractive modern building which bore this name and knew that it was a branch of the Pentecostal church, but that was all. Paul Snow continued, 'We used to be Anglicans but we now go to Elim. I'm not saying it'll necessarily be right for you but we really do welcome people whoever they are and whatever their situation.'

'All right, I might try Elim,' I said.

It was late when I got into bed but I couldn't sleep for some time. I no longer felt alone. Paul Snow had prayed that God would be with me, and I knew he was. Not the vague, impersonal being I'd been picturing for most of my life. But a personal, practical, caring, involved God.

I had no doubts at all now about the rightness of my decision. I would stand by Geoff and God's presence with me would make all the difference.

My burdens had not all been lifted and I still felt bruised and battered emotionally, but I sensed that something new was beginning; that the pressure had lightened a little.

The next day I kept my appointment with Mr Bowden and told him that I would not be separating from or divorcing my husband. Now I knew that these were not the right courses of action, nor what I wanted to do. I intended instead, with God's help, to go on loving and caring for Geoff.

Mr Bowden responded with his usual quiet friendliness.

The rest of the day was very busy as I got the four of us ready to go away the following morning. When packing for myself, I included my Bible – hoping desperately that in it I would discover more about this God who was real and close and interested in every detail of our lives.

On arrival at Dartmouth, I was exhausted. The weather was hot and sunny. With no meals to cook or housework to do I was able, with Craig, to go for walks in lovely surroundings and enjoy the river and boats. There was time, too, to read my Bible and pray – my prayers being mainly cries for help.

As gently as I could I told Craig a little more about Geoff. He was upset but it was good that he was able to express his feelings and talk about what had happened. He also wrote a letter to Geoff – saying that he missed him and hoped he'd be home soon – and made him a card. I found it heartbreaking to see these things and knew Geoff would be deeply affected when he received them.

Then, just as the peace and beauty all around were beginning to have a soothing effect, the phone rang.

It was my parents to say that the West Mercia police had asked to search my house and so they had had to hand over a key. The police had also wanted to know where I was and had said they would be in touch with me.

All the good caused by the last few restful days was immediately undone. Evidently the Hereford police had handed the case over to the West Mercia Division. That indicated that things were looking more serious.

On the next day, Thursday, Detective Chief Superintendent Cole of West Mercia's CID telephoned me.

Preliminaries over, he said, 'I'm afraid we need you back for questioning.'

My heart sank but I managed to muster just enough spirit to reply, 'I'll be back next week.'

'I'm sorry, Mrs Prime, but it's urgent. We'll come and pick you up if you like.'

'No,' I said, even more resolutely. 'I need this break and I'm not going back home in the middle of it.'

'I appreciate how you feel but we really must see you.'

In the end, I settled reluctantly for a compromise. We would meet at Paignton Police Station on Friday.

I telephoned my parents to tell them what had happened, and they said they would come down for the weekend.

On Friday, while mum looked after Craig, dad and I went to the police station. There, for over four hours, I was grilled about my life. Many of the questions were highly personal. I supposed they wouldn't be asking me these things unless they really needed to; even so, I grew more and more upset and resentful.

I realise now that I, like Geoff, was under suspicion but I still wonder whether it was really necessary to put me through so much suffering.

Afterwards I was too exhausted and churned up to enjoy the rest of the holiday. Between us we tried to give Craig a good time, though.

For me the only highlight was a helpful sermon heard in a Methodist Church on Sunday. Aptly enough, it was about Onesimus in prison – a topic I'd never heard anyone speak on before.

The next day we drove home, gathering up Mark and Stephen on the way.

It was evening when we arrived and discovered what had happened in our absence.

Evidently the police had removed much of our electrical equipment. Craig was upset to find that even his toy electric car, a present from his father, had gone. Stephen and Mark were dismayed that the stereo set had been taken and I doubted whether they were satisfied with my vague explanation that the police had had to check on something.

Sick at heart, I went up to one of the boys' bedrooms. On the floor was a large pair of shoes and over the chair a blue boiler suit.

Have they been sleeping here? I wondered.

I put the question to them when they arrived not long afterwards.

Yes, they had, they said. I felt cross. Was this further invasion of our privacy really necessary? They explained what they had taken and asked me to sign for the items. I did so.

'Mrs Prime, please don't tell your boys yet what this is all about,' they said.

'But Stephen and Mark know something strange is going on. I can't keep fobbing them off indefinitely,' I replied.

'If you can rely on them completely not to say a word to anyone else, then you can tell them. But not otherwise, please,' they said.

At last the police left us to unpack and go to bed. When Craig was in bed, I told Mark and Stephen that I had something dreadful to tell them. Looking very concerned, they waited for me to continue. Once again I had the hateful task of conveying shattering news to my children. I told them that the police were investigating the more than likely possibility that Geoff had been a spy.

They said little, but their shocked and anxious expressions told me everything. Soon after this the three of us had to go to bed, but I doubt whether any of us slept much that night.

For the next weeks, the police were frequent visitors, calling to question me and search the house at any hour of the day and sometimes late at night.

The boys went back to school on Tuesday and I contacted Paul Snow, who arranged to pick me up and take me to meet his wife June a day or so later. The trauma of the past few days had left me close to desperation, although the peace I had experienced had not disappeared altogether.

Paul Snow arrived, as previously arranged, at about eleven o'clock in the morning, and we got into his dark-coloured Estate car. He inserted the key into its slot and turned it. Nothing happened. He tried again and again. Still nothing happened.

'Oh well, we'll just have to pray about it,' he said cheerfully.

To my utter amazement, he proceeded to ask the Almighty to help get the car started. Then he turned the key again. There was still no response from the engine.

My heart sank and a prayer formed in my mind: *Don't let me down now – not after raising my hopes.*

Paul prayed again and again – to no effect.

Growing desperate, I said, 'You'd be welcome to have coffee in my house,' but even as I spoke I realised that this didn't solve the problem of June waiting for us at their home – no doubt anxiously by now, and with the coffee getting cold.

'Don't worry,' said Paul. 'We'll sort this out. It's an attack of the devil.' I must have looked startled but he continued, 'We often have an attack when we are trying to do something for God. I broke down on the motorway several times last night, but I got home in the end, with much prayer.'

While I was digesting this, he added, 'We're asking God for another car. One that keeps breaking down isn't good enough for his work.'

I was dumbstruck.

'All right, Lord,' Paul said, conversationally, 'I'm going to pray one more time. Otherwise we'll have to do something else.'

He got out of the driving seat, went round to front of the car and raised the bonnet. I joined him there. Laying his hands on the engine, Paul prayed. I stood by feeling rather embarrassed. He would look such a fool when the car refused yet again to start!

We returned to our seats and Paul turned the ignition key.

The engine sputtered into life and we were off with a burst of 'Thank you, Lord. Hallelujah!' from the driver. The joy he so clearly felt was beyond me just then, but I was amazed – and relieved.

After a short drive, Paul stopped outside a Victorian-style house and said, 'Here we are.'

13

Confession

June Snow greeted us warmly, taking our delay and the cause of it very much in her stride. She showed me into a large, attractively furnished lounge and brought in coffee and biscuits on a tray. The warmth and friendliness of the couple helped me to relax. They spoke of their Christian faith and their work with the FGBMFI and I found myself listening eagerly.

Coffee over, Paul said gently, 'We'd better begin at the beginning hadn't we?' Because I felt accepted and cared for by these people, I was able to put into words the pain, guilt and resentment I was carrying as a result of my first marriage and the divorce. They listened very intently, asking an occasional question. At last it was all out.

Paul said, 'Before we go any further we need to do something about all this.' Turning to June he asked, 'Do you agree that we should pray now about the past?'

'Yes,' she said. 'Let's stand in a circle and join hands.' We stood and linked hands, then Paul said, 'June and I will pray, Rhona, and if you want to as well, please do. If you'd rather join in silently, that'll be all right, too.'

Paul prayed, with confidence and authority, that God would completely forgive all the wrongs of the past and heal all its hurts.

I had a tremendous sense of relief. June prayed next – that God would protect me from all evil, harmful influences. I started to cry but now they were healing tears.

Paul said, 'We can talk now about the present.'

I told them more about the situation I was in and, because of their accepting, unjudging attitude, felt able to speak freely and ask questions.

'I've been studying the Bible a little,' I told them, 'and feel confused about who I'm supposed to be married to in the sight of God.'

'You're married to Geoff,' Paul responded. 'That's your present situation. So what do you want to ask God for in that situation?'

The answers becoming immediately clear to me, I said, 'I would love Geoff to become a committed Christian and know this peace and forgiveness too. And I just want him back as head of the household, where he should be.'

'All right,' Paul said. 'The Bible says that if two or three are gathered in Jesus's name, he's there with them, and that if two Christians agree about something and pray in faith and according to God's will for it, they will receive it. There are three of us here and we can agree together about this and pray in faith and confidence.'

Holding hands, we prayed very earnestly for Geoff. Once again the pressure inside me eased as I felt my burdens being shared.

Afterwards June brought in more coffee. Then Paul and June prayed for me, the boys, the rest of the family and our total situation. All the time, I was learning more of this caring, confident and specific way of praying. One by one my problems and concerns were talked through with this God who now seemed so near and real. I felt supported by him and by my new friends.

Afterwards, I cried tears of joy. Paul and June hugged me and thanked God for what he had done and would do in my life. I couldn't help joining in.

Then Paul asked, 'Where does all this leave you, Rhona?'

'With a new vision and hope,' I replied unhesitatingly.

In the coming days I discovered that I was still the same person – weak and sinful, at the end of my physical and emotional tether and suffering all the natural consequences – which, for me, meant losing weight, feeling sick at the sight of food, sleeping poorly and getting easily agitated. But now I fully grasped for the first time that God cared about *me* and that I could have a personal daily relationship with him.

My situation remained unchanged too. But I had begun to see it in a new way – not simply as a horrific, disastrous mess, but as something God knew all about, and from which – now that I had stopped trying to run my own life and had asked him to take charge – he could and would bring good.

On the following Sunday, I went to the Elim church with Craig who felt he wanted to come along too. The friendly atmosphere soon put me at my ease. When the service began I was caught up in worshipping God and able to forget about myself. The songs were easy to pick up and everyone seemed to be singing wholeheartedly. The talk was from the Bible, practical and in everyday language.

Craig and I had both enjoyed the service and we decided to attend regularly. We soon made new friends and Mr Glass, the minister, took a great interest in our family and became a wise and trusted counsellor to us.

One Sunday I invited Stephen and Mark to go to church with Craig and me.

'No way,' they said. 'That's where all the weird people go.'

'That's your opinion,' I said. 'But I like it a lot and if ever you do want to come, you'd be very welcome.'

Due to having been away and various pressures I hadn't visited Geoff for three weeks. It was about the middle of June when I did manage to do so again.

My husband was in a very bad state. On the previous Wednesday, June 8th, the West Mercia police had asked to see him, he said. My heart was in my mouth as I heard him add that they had produced his wallet and its contents and had started questioning him about it.

'I told them that I had had contacts with the Russians, but had not been a spy,' he told me.

I was thrown into panic and confusion. Did he know I had given the wallet to the police? Evidently not, but I simply couldn't tell him. And what was I to make of what he had told the police? If *that* was the truth, had he been lying or fantasising to me on that dreadful night before his arrest? If not – what would be the outcome?

Geoff then told me that Dr Hall, a psychiatrist, had seen him and had outlined a possible course of treatment.

I went away from the visit, my thoughts in chaos again, and lived through another wretched week – torn between acute anxiety for Geoff and dread that he would discover my part in what he was going through. But at the next visit he said nothing about any further interviews and I didn't bring the matter up. Instead we talked about our different situations and I noticed the marks on his thumbs caused by the work he was doing – sewing mailbags by hand.

The suspense of the next few days and nights became almost intolerable. Were the police continuing to question Geoff, I kept wondering. What would he be telling them? Prayer, the Bible, Christian friends and gatherings became my vital lifelines.

It was on the afternoon of Sunday, June 27th, that the police telephoned. Could they see me?

'I'm going to church soon,' I said. 'Could you come afterwards?'

They agreed.

At eight o'clock the doorbell rang. On the doorstep were Mr Picken and Mr Cole. One look at their unsmiling faces was enough to set my heart thumping even before they asked, 'Could we see you in private?'

My parents and the boys being in the lounge, I showed them into the kitchen. As we stood there, Detective Chief Superintendent Cole said, 'Your husband has asked us to come and tell you personally that he has confessed fully to espionage.'

The question I had been living with for so long had been finally and shatteringly answered. Geoff had been a spy and had told the authorities so. As these facts were registering, Mr Cole continued, 'He finished making his statement this afternoon. It's an extremely long one and I'm afraid things look serious.'

Dread was added to my other feelings but I had to ask,

'Have you any idea how long he will get?' – whether desperately hoping that things would be better than I feared or unable to bear the suspense of not knowing the worst, I'm not sure.

The men said that they'd rather not say, they couldn't be sure, and they might be years out either way. But I kept pestering them. Eventually they said, 'You'd better sit down.' I collapsed on to a seat and waited, in excruciating suspense. Reluctantly they hazarded a guess at twenty-five years!

I doubled up and started to cry. It was a nightmare figure which I wanted to reject but couldn't altogether.

After I had regained some outward semblance of control they told me of how Geoff had been questioned. He had admitted nothing at first and then on the previous day had confessed to everything, starting with the words: 'Yes, Mr Cole, at four o'clock today, June 26th, I now wish to tell you the truth of this tragic affair. I cannot go on talking about my wife whilst I am continuing to tell lies. It will take a long time . . .' It had taken nine hours.

Having delivered this desolating news, the police told me that they needed to search the loft for a miniature camera.

'Your husband has told us where he thinks it is,' they said.

I gave my permission, while inwardly seething at the insensitivity of the men. After what I had just heard I was in no fit state to cope with their continued presence.

As soon as they'd gone upstairs, I fled to the lounge and, after the boys had tactfully withdrawn, gave rein to my emotions. Rather incoherently, I told my parents what had taken place. They did their best to help me, while obviously being desperately upset themselves. I tried to think about what to say to the boys. Stephen and Mark would have to be given the facts but I wanted to say as little as possible to Craig for the moment.

It was nearly eleven o'clock by the time the police left and I was able to crawl into bed, the boys having gone up earlier. My parents, very concerned about me, decided to sleep in our lounge rather than return to their home for the night.

The next day, nearly nine weeks after his arrest, Geoff was formally committed for trial on a charge of three sexual offences at Hereford Magistrates' Court. So there was fresh hurt, humiliation and exposure for us all. Days and nights were one long struggle against overwhelming odds.

The police were frequent callers either in person or on the phone, as they continued to question me and search our home. They combed the loft repeatedly and also searched all the bedrooms – looking under floorboards and in cavity walls. One day we had ten of them about the place, looking everywhere – including the roof – and using special equipment from London. They even, to my acute dismay, had to question the boys about the camera, but this never came to light.

It was a gruelling time. Without God and the practical and financial help of parents and friends, we wouldn't, I believe, have survived. As it was I didn't fall apart completely and the boys were amazing, considering what they were going through. Mark and Stephen had school exams to cope with. How relatively unimportant they seemed!

The car, returned earlier by the police, was now being made ready for sale by a garage. As well as sorting out the tyre, they were having to repair the driver's seat.

Like the car, our bedroom was associated with unbearable memories. I felt I couldn't stand the décor any longer, and charged round buying paint, wallpaper and curtain material, and trying to find a decorator whom I could afford. This bout of activity exhausted me – but not nearly as much as did my ordeal early in July.

Then, the police asked me to make a detailed statement about Geoff. As a wife I needn't do this, they said, but I was advised to cooperate. In the end, very reluctantly, I did.

Thirty-one pages of statement and many hours later, I collapsed into bed and stayed there for three days feeling really ill, while others kindly took over my responsibilities. The mental agony resulting from that experience lasted many months. It was sheer torture being grilled about someone I loved, and I am still harrowed by the memory of it all.

Geoff and I at this time were like a couple of wounded animals with hardly the strength to lick our own wounds, let alone one another's. But one good thing that happened to Geoff was that he was interviewed by another psychiatrist, someone named Dr Marks, to whom he related particularly well and whom he hoped to see again.

Meanwhile, we both lived in dread of the storm that was about to burst. One day Geoff was informed that he'd be moved to Winson Green in Birmingham, but no one would say when this would happen. Already frustrated by the noise, lack of time and privacy at our meetings, he now faced an uncertain future, in which things were likely to get worse. He was particularly worried about how and when I would be able to visit him at Winson Green.

In desperation, he went to see the Deputy Governor. This man understood the problem and kindly arranged for Geoff and me to have a long morning visit on a Wednesday in the middle of July.

On the Monday before the visit I made arrangements for the car to be advertised for sale in the local paper on the Wednesday. Soon afterwards Mr Picken rang to ask whether he and Detective Chief Superintendent Mayo – whom I had previously met in connection with making my statement – could come and see me regarding further developments in my husband's case. With a very heavy heart, fearing the worst, I made arrangements for them to come at lunchtime the following day.

Within minutes of their arrival Mr Picken was saying, 'Your husband is about to be charged under the Official Secrets Act and remanded awaiting trial, and he will shortly be transferred to Winson Green Prison. I'm afraid the press will really go to town on this story, and you and your family will need to get right away for a while.'

I sat there, panic-stricken, as they went on to explain in more detail what would be happening. They also told me that I would need police protection for my home and offered to take me to Gloucester Prison for the visit to Geoff on Wednesday.

The rest of the day passed in frantic activity. Dazed though I was, I had to arrange for our stay with relatives in Cheshire from Thursday onwards, cancel the milk and papers, pack, ring the boys' schools to ask leave of absence and explain the situation, and contact social security, solicitors, Mr Glass, neighbours and friends . . .

I told Stephen and Mark when they returned from school that the story was about to break and what had been arranged. Then there was the difficult task of explaining things to Craig. He was dreadfully upset. How much he really grasped at that point about the spying, I'm not sure but he certainly understood that Geoff had done something very wrong and would be in prison for a longer time than we had anticipated.

Dread of the unknown future dominated my feelings but there was one comforting thought: tomorrow, at last, I would be able to have a longer, more personal visit with Geoff.

14

Exposure

Wednesday morning came and, as arranged, a member of West Mercia's police force came to pick us up – Mark, my eldest son, having decided to come and support me. On the drive to Gloucester, I discovered to my joy that our driver was a Christian. This fact and his friendly courtesy were a real bonus to me as I approached the visit to Geoff which I believed would be a crucial one. When we arrived at the prison, the driver and Mark waited outside while I was taken to see my husband.

For the first time since his arrest, we found ourselves able to talk more freely, sharing our burdens and trying to help one another. There was, however, a very heavy burden which I still kept from Geoff – that of my 'betrayal' of him. I still believed that the decision which I'd taken had been right – but that didn't stop me grieving for my husband or being assailed by pangs of guilt and self-recrimination. And I still shrank from telling him what I had done.

We discussed the forthcoming publicity – both hating the thought of all the probable exposure and being in complete agreement about having as little to do with the press and media as possible.

After the visit, we were due to see the Cheltenham police but as this would now have to wait until after lunch, our policeman-driver kindly took Mark and myself out for a quick bite to eat and then drove us to the police station where we entered into discussions about the security arrangements that were to be made with regard to our home. Then we were driven home and, some time later, a security man arrived to check doors and windows and fit an alarm system. Also several people rang to enquire about the car, in response to the advertisement, and I sold it to the first person to see and make a satisfactory cash offer for it.

The next day, all the arrangements having, somehow, been completed, the boys and I were picked up by dad in his car and set off for Cheshire. It was reassuring to know that while we were away, our home would be under continuous police protection.

But no one could provide us with emotional protection, and as we travelled along we were lacerated by the words of the announcer broadcast over the car radio: 'Mr G. A. Prime of Laburnham Cottage, Pittville Crescent Lane, Cheltenham, has been charged under the Official Secrets Act. He is accused that between January 1st, 1968, and December 31st, 1981, in England, for a purpose prejudicial to the safety and interests of the state, he communicated to other persons information which was calculated to be, or might be, or was intended to be, directly or indirectly, useful to the enemy.'

Afterwards, the agony inside the car was almost tangible. Everything else about that journey – the weather, the traffic, even stopping for lunch – is blurred in my memory.

We arrived at the home of our relatives in Cheshire by mid afternoon. Their welcome was loving and kind.

The next thing that stands out clearly in my mind happened while we were watching the news on television at teatime. Suddenly, there on the screen, looking desperately haggard and morose, was Geoff. The next moment the voice of a television newsreader was reading out the charges against him. Craig's cousin took him quickly and quietly out of the room while I broke down and cried. After a moment, unable to bear any more, I asked for the television to be turned off. It was, but our anguish could not be.

My dilemma in the next days was acute. Should I read the papers and watch the news or not? I wanted to know what was happening to Geoff, but every picture, article and announcement was heartbreaking.

Soon after arriving back at his home, dad rang. There were, he said, people from the media all over Cheltenham desperate for a story. They had been hounding my family, friends and neighbours. I heard later that they were besieging Geoff's family too, and those with whom he'd worked in Cheltenham.

I felt alarmed and depressed by this news.

In other circumstances our family would have revelled in the holiday we were being given. As it was, it helped us to survive. Our relations were wonderful, taking us for walks or driving us to beauty spots. We picnicked and the boys swam and played tennis.

Every day I read my Bible and prayed, looking desperately for promises to cling to.

We couldn't stay away for ever. On Monday, after a week and a half away, we returned to Laburnham Cottage, my parents having previously checked that there were no press-men about and only two friendly policemen on guard at the gates. Soon afterwards Mr Bowden came to the house and helped me to frame a short statement for the press, hoping that it would put a stop once and for all to their pestering of us and others.

Mr Bowden rang some of the hotels in Cheltenham and learnt that only a reporter from the *Gloucestershire Echo* was available – the representatives of the other papers having left that morning. When the remaining reporter arrived, my solicitor went out and read him my statement which said that I and my family had been greatly saddened by what had happened and that I would have nothing more to say until after the trial at the very earliest.

Next day the newsmen – presumably having been given the tip-off about my return home – were back in full force. There were reporters and photographers from most if not all the main newspapers and magazines, ranging from the cheap tabloids to the quality glossies, as well as freelance journalists and photographers and book publishers. Radio and television networks were well represented too.

Some sat outside the gate in cars, waiting for anyone to

emerge from our house. When we did they would leap out and surge forward, snapping cameras for all they were worth. Others rang the doorbell to ask for interviews. Once when I was standing at the front door talking to someone, I suddenly realised that a cameraman, half-hidden behind a bush, was photographing me.

Being ex-directory, I thought we were safe from the telephone. But a reporter got hold of our number through having a drink with someone who happened to have one of Geoff's personal cards. Geoff had had these printed, with name, address and phone number, when working for the wine company.

Having achieved this little scoop the reporter rang to ask me whether I would pose for some photos. Polite but firm, I said that I would not. Other phone calls followed. Our secret number was secret no longer.

I tried to think calm, understanding thoughts about these people. They were, after all, only doing their job. But when I found myself having to crawl round my lounge for a couple of days in order to avoid the zoom lens camera that was angled to 'see' right into our front room, I grew very annoyed. Surely the freedom of the press was too free if it could ride roughshod over people's wishes and feelings – particularly during their times of suffering. And what right had they to invade the privacy of my family, friends and neighbours? What had they done to deserve that?

One man said he'd keep coming back. From now on, he told me, any new situation in my life would be known about. Even if I moved away the press would find out where I'd gone.

Insulted, I thought: *Anyone would think I was a piece of public property!* But his words were to prove horrifyingly true.

Another day, accompanied by one of the policemen guarding the house, I went to a parked car to tell the man inside that he was making life very difficult for us by hanging around and to ask him to drive off and leave us in peace.

Before I had finished speaking, he leapt out of the car, camera in hand, and started taking pictures of me while retorting. '*You're* the one who's being difficult by not letting us take pictures or giving us interviews. If you gave us what we wanted, we'd go away.'

Angry and upset, I rushed back to the house.

The police on guard worked in twos, doing four-hour stints at a time, all through the day and night. They were pleasant and helpful. We took tea out and talked to some of them. The decorator, who had begun work on the bedroom soon after our return, took exception to being stopped and questioned at the gate every time he came to the house, but fortunately he kept coming until, to my immense relief, he had completely transformed the room.

One midday, a policeman in plain clothes called to tell me that the guard would be removed as from teatime that day.

'But why?' I asked, feeling suddenly very apprehensive and vulnerable. 'The press are still coming and I need you here.' His answers were vague at first but with a little persistence I managed to uncover the facts.

Someone representing a newspaper had rung the police to say that if the guards were not removed from our house, they'd run a story about how public money was being wasted in this way.

I felt very disturbed at this example of the power of the press, as well as concerned at our unprotected state. In ironic contrast to our situation IRA 'super-grasses' and their families nowadays are given massive day and night police protection.

In the absence of human guards I had to rely even more on God and he kept me safe and helped me to do all things I needed to do each day.

I bought a second-hand car – a harvest gold Mini. The money I had received from selling our old car, plus a small gift, exactly covered the cost of buying and insuring it. I couldn't drive it as yet but driving lessons continued, with the help of family and friends – who also drove me wherever I needed to go and later, by servicing the Mini for me, among other things, enabled me to keep it on the road. I came to think of it as God's car – provided by him and for his use.

I was visiting the doctor regularly. He thought I was coping well, considering. But I wasn't too sure, as my sleeplessness and weight loss were ongoing problems and I was now worried about getting anorexia nervosa. The agitation was also very bad at times, giving me 'the shakes'.

The doctor prescribed as best he could while admitting, 'They don't make pills for a situation like this. You're in the World Cup class right now.'

I'd have given a great deal to be out of that class and back as a housewife coping with the normal ups and downs of family life! Some people would do anything, good or bad, to get into the limelight. For Geoff, the experience was excruciating. I remembered his telling me once how he loved London because he could merge and mingle there unnoticed and unknown. While disliking that sort of anonymity, I too hated the idea of strangers knowing my private business. So I doubt whether anyone could have found a more reluctant couple than Geoff and I were, to face the glare of publicity.

But I had the support and help of friends and neighbours as well as the presence of God. He seemed to be saying to me in different ways, *I'm still here, Rhona, and I always will be. I'll meet your needs and those of your family. Trust me. Don't lose heart.*

The boys were helpful and thoughtful, too. They never left me in the house alone if they could help it, and took on extra jobs. Stephen and Mark, being tall and strong, were useful in all kinds of ways and I felt less vulnerable when they were around for protection. Craig and Geoff had always done the vegetable garden together. Craig now said he would keep doing it for Geoff until he came out of prison! He made a good job of it too.

Equally important and helpful to me was the fact that the boys accepted my decision to stand by Geoff and decided to do the same – in their different ways.

Thanks to newspaper and television coverage, 'Prime' was a name which turned people's heads. It was a new and painful experience for me to see people react when I said who I was. I was beginning to be recognised in shops or walking along the streets. It was unnerving to sense that I was being looked at or talked about by people I didn't know, whose reactions I could only guess at.

I met Jane regularly. Once after seeing Geoff on television she said, 'Do get him to change that red shirt, Rhona. People will think he's flaunting his beliefs.'

How ironic! I thought, knowing that it was I who had persuaded a very reluctant husband to buy the garment in question.

Geoff's life in Winson Green Prison contrasted sharply with mine at home. As I was later to discover, he was anxious about many things – not least the fact that I hadn't seen him for a fortnight. Towards the end of the month I did at last manage a visit.

15

Tension

Seen from the outside Winson Green was enough to strike gloom into anyone's heart. Mum and I were about to see it. We were sitting in a police car being driven by a member of West Mercia's CID, on our way to visit Geoff.

An hour after first setting out, we found ourselves passing through a depressed area of Birmingham. Before long we came within sight of the prison walls. They were brick built, though grime had obscured most of the original red – and forbiddingly tall and thick.

In the parking area in front of the prison, our driver stopped to identify himself to a prison officer, who then told him where to park.

A moment later we were walking towards huge wood-and-metal gates, in which a smaller door had been cut. The CID man lifted then banged down the metal knocker. Almost immediately it opened and a guard looked out. He asked our business and checked our driver's identification before allowing us to step inside.

We found ourselves in an enclosed courtyard beyond which, behind more locked gates, lay the prison buildings. We were admitted to the main entrance – a huge area with offices to left and right. There our business was explained once again. Having listened, the prison officer radioed through for two other officials: one to take Geoff to the meeting room and the other to escort me there. Then he asked to see what I had brought.

I held up my bag and he looked over the contents, then

directed us to the waiting room and asked whether we'd like a cup of tea. We accepted gratefully and went to the room indicated.

It was small with grime-grey walls and barred windows draped with dingy net curtains. On one window-sill there were a couple of dead or dying pot-plants. We seated ourselves on three of the unoccupied metal-and-canvas chairs which, like the central table, were decidedly the worse for wear.

I guessed that the room would have been considerably noisier and fuller had this been a normal visiting time. As it was, there were only a few others present and these, I thought, would be solicitors or others on official business rather than relatives of the prisoners.

A man in prison uniform came in carrying the tea. I discovered later that he was a 'trusty' – a prisoner nearing the end of his sentence and considered trustworthy enough to do certain jobs.

I sipped from my cup and thought about Geoff. How would he cope with living in this grim place and with being so far away from us?

An officer entered and said with a smile, 'Mrs Prime?'

'Yes,' I said.

'Will you come this way, please?' he invited.

I said a quick goodbye to mum and the driver, then followed the man through the door, across a courtyard, past the large inner gates – unlocked to admit us and relocked afterwards – and down a path to the right. Prison officers and guard dogs were on patrol nearby. Another door lay ahead of us. Once again we had to knock and wait for clearance before being admitted to what lay on the other side.

The scene which greeted us etched itself permanently on my memory.

The setting was a small garden with an immaculate lawn bordered by well-tended flowerbeds bursting with summer colours. The scent of the blooms was in the air and I could hear birds singing nearby.

In stark, tragic contrast was a group of prisoners out on

exercise. With their shuffling gait, drooping shoulders and downcast looks, they presented a picture of utter despair. Some, I noticed with an added pang, were very young.

'What a terrible sight!' I murmured, when the prisoners and their guards had moved out of earshot.

'Yes,' my escort agreed imperturbably. 'They're from the hospital wing, I think.'

No doubt he'd seen it all before, but it had caught me on the raw. Somehow, though, I would have to block it from my mind for the moment and rally myself for the coming visit.

'Where are we going?' I asked.

'To the morgue,' the officer replied, adding, when he saw the panic on my face, 'Don't worry, it's not used for that now. It just happens to be the only place available at the moment for you to visit your husband.'

Leaving the garden behind us, we entered a small brick hut and went along a stone passage. Some prison officers were there. One of them removed the contents of my carrier bag, telling me the things would be examined and delivered later. Then he indicated a room to the left.

I went inside. Geoff was sitting at a table. His posture and expression spelt total dejection. Rather tearfully, we hugged and kissed each other.

I sat down opposite him, noticing that he was wearing the prison uniform of brown trousers and a blue-and-white striped shirt under a brown jacket.

We started to talk about what we had been doing since we last met. Geoff spoke of his nightmarish journey from Gloucester in a police van with a huge police escort and sirens screaming through all the towns. He was locked up on his own for twenty-three hours out of every twenty-four and had nothing to do all day except read and think. During the remaining hour he was allowed to exercise in a small yard with three guards watching him.

No wonder he was gloomy, I thought.

I told him a little about what had been happening to us.

'The boys are wanting to see you,' I said. 'But I keep stalling – because I'm worried about the effects on them.'

'I'd like to see them, but I'm not sure I could cope with them yet either,' he said.

We spoke of the press – still in complete agreement about not giving interviews to anyone.

The hour was soon up and I had to leave. There had been so much left unsaid and we'd both been conscious of the guard sitting just outside the door.

The first of August was a red-letter day for Craig and me. It was a Sunday and during the evening service, he became a Christian. Simply and sincerely, he prayed that Jesus Christ would come into his life and save and help him.

I was almost as excited as Craig himself. For some time I'd been praying that my whole household would come to know God, and here was my first answer! Craig's faith was a great help to him and an encouragement to me in the days ahead.

Not long afterwards, while Geoff was still being given the morgue as his visiting room, I agreed to take Mark to Winson Green. He coped with all the preliminaries well enough but I still felt apprehensive as I sat outside with the guards while Mark and Geoff had a time together.

Mark told me later that he had been very worried about what to say, but after he and Geoff had shaken hands, he'd felt more relaxed and the two of them had had a good talk.

Then it was my turn to see Geoff and Mark's to sit with the guards.

When we met up again, Mark told me that he'd had a long and interesting talk with them about being a prison warder. I felt relieved – and grateful, having prayed hard about this meeting. Far from being a harmful experience for Mark, it had proved instructive and stimulating.

Geoff had very few visitors from outside. His parents had died long before and his two brothers and one step-sister appeared to be writing him off. One brother, urged on and brought from Staffordshire by two female members of the press, presumably hoping for a story, did visit him once. As his brother talked about how he'd managed to come, my husband's suspicions were immediately aroused.

'Try and think of Rhona and the boys,' he told him. 'And don't trust any of the press.'

We had visited this brother occasionally and evidently Geoff felt that mentioning us would carry some weight. At any rate, we never heard from him again though we tried to contact him.

16

Time of waiting

It was during a visit in August, while my husband was still in
the old morgue, that I managed to make the admission which
I'd been putting off for almost three months.

Geoff spoke that day about how, prior to the police
interrogating him about spying and producing his wallet, he
had begun to feel optimistic – his sexual problems being out
in the open at last and a possible course of treatment
suggested; and his espionage being, as far as he was concerned, a thing of the past. He'd already written, he said, to
the London office of the examining body for the Wine and
Spirits trade and, with our proposed wine shop in mind, had
actually been studying their textbook when he'd been called
out for the interview by the police.

I felt I couldn't put off the moment of confession any longer
but with the agonising question in my mind: *Will this be the
end between us?* it was appallingly hard to admit that it was I
who had handed over the wallet to the police.

Seeing my husband's expression, my heart sank like a
stone but I plunged on, as tears filled my eyes, 'I just felt it
was right for everyone's sake. We had to tell the truth and
wipe the slate clean. You could never be a whole person with
that on your conscience.'

He put his hands over mine and gave me a comforting
squeeze. My tears flowed faster, but with relief now.

'You're probably right,' he was saying. 'We couldn't have
had a future with all that kept back. There's been more than

90

enough deceit in the past. I don't blame you for what you did and understand why you felt you had to do it.'

It was an emotionally draining visit, but I came away feeling very relieved that Geoff now knew what I had done, and touched at his reaction.

School holidays brought extra busyness. I seemed to have to spend much time phoning officials or filling in forms in connection with social security and other matters to do with Geoff's situation or ours. Then there were driving lessons, friends, other letters and phone calls, the church and church meetings . . .

Summer faded and the golds and russets of autumn transfigured the landscape.

My weekly visits to Geoff continued. It was a great help to be driven to and from Winson Green Prison by the police, and I always found them and the prison officials courteous and helpful. On entering the waiting room one day I had a pleasant surprise. The once dingy place had been transformed by a new coat of paint. In contrast, I was badly shocked by my first sight of the interior of the main prison complex, where I began to visit Geoff in September.

Just before being taken to the new visiting room I stood at the edge of the central well of the building. Above me was a series of spiralling staircases and corridors. The stark grimness of the place and the thought of so many human beings packed into cells, storey by storey, filled me with gloom and compassion. A moment later, I was taken to see Geoff and had to focus on all the things I needed to ask him or talk about.

Our meetings varied during that time. Some were very fraught – others less so. Through them and our letters, we both tried to sort out family matters and build a relationship.

One day Dr Marks, the psychiatrist, saw my husband again and said there'd be another interview some time. These interviews were for the primary purpose of making out a report, but Geoff found them a help and in time seemed more able to talk with me about his childhood and other personal matters. I hoped that after the trial he would really start receiving the help he needed and wanted.

Mark visited Geoff again, this time accompanied by Stephen. They had a good time together and I felt this was another hurdle negotiated.

On October 1st, Geoff was taken to Hereford Magistrates' Court yet again and committed for trial on a charge of espionage. The actual trial was to take place on November 29th at the Central Criminal Court, known as The Old Bailey. Predictably the press converged on us. Interest was not now just nationwide, but worldwide, and the United States was particularly involved, since their National Security Agency and our GCHQ had been working together on certain projects affecting the USSR. The Americans were none too pleased that someone working at GCHQ had been giving information to the Soviet Union about these projects and many were critical about British Security procedures and angry at not being informed earlier about the case.

Increasingly the trial occupied my thoughts. At times it seemed incredible that my husband would be tried at the highest court in the land, but at other times the horrendous reality of what was to happen in less than two months' time was all too clear to me.

Should I go to the trial or not? That was one pressing question. Some of my family and friends were anxious about my going and I, too, wanted to shrink from all the pain and publicity. But the conviction grew that I would have to go – if only for Geoff's sake.

My friend Jane immediately offered to go with me and made the necessary arrangements with her colleagues. Later, Mr Hirst, the Anglican vicar who had been visiting Geoff and who, I'd discovered to my amazement, was a friend of Mr Bowden, my solicitor, said he'd like to attend the trial, too, by way of support for us.

Clothes were not a priority in my life at the time, but I did wonder what I should wear at the trial and felt that I should make an effort to be suitably dressed for the occasion. Under the impression that in London everyone wore hats, I went out to buy one. Jane accompanied me. I told her that I was thinking of something plain and perhaps grey in colour.

In between looking for and trying on hats we talked, among other things, about our long and intermittent friendship.

'Whenever you disappeared out of my life without a word, I'd be pretty sure that you were off again, doing your own thing, your way, without consulting God or anyone else – and that sooner or later things would go wrong!' she told me, and I laughed ruefully.

We saw a great many hats I didn't like or couldn't afford, before catching sight of a light grey trilby style one. I tried it on and Jane and I both agreed that it was just right. I noticed a Biro mark on the brim and pointed this out to the assistant, who, accordingly, reduced the price. I bought the hat.

What to wear with it was another problem, my clothes being far too big due to my continuing weight loss. I looked through a mail order catalogue and sent off for a suit which looked smart. There was still the question of how to pay for it when it arrived. My parents, I knew, would give me the money if I asked for it, but I preferred to try to manage without having to do that. As well as praying, I tried to sell some of our things: a few of Geoff's clothes, his squash racquet, a camera, a cassette recorder, an old television set and some furniture.

It was a testing time, but God was with me – unforgettably so at a meeting which I attended one day. It was another of the gatherings run by the organisation involving Paul and June Snow and others whom I knew – the FGBMFI. Once again, I was caught up in the atmosphere of worship and joy.

Afterwards, with others, I went forward to ask for prayer. A group of leaders, including Paul, came over to where I was standing. I found myself sobbing painfully as they placed their hands on my head and began to pray for me.

The next thing I knew, I was lying on the floor, feeling

utterly at peace, crying tears of joy, and under the impression that I was surrounded by angels.

As full awareness returned, I realised that the 'angels' were people – one of these being my mother – standing or kneeling around me and praying.

Nothing like that had ever happened to me before, but I was completely unhurt and unafraid – certain that God was very close to me and that the experience and the peace had come from him.

Slowly I got to my feet. People came and spoke to me – loving, encouraging words. One of them was Paul. He said, 'I have some verses from the Bible which I believe are for you.'

Looking down at his open Bible he read: 'God chose the weak things of the world to shame the strong. He chose the lowly things of this world and the despised things – and things that are not – to nullify the things that are, so that no one can boast before him.'

Then he looked at me and said, 'I believe God will use you in an amazing way, and that you will be like a light across the nation in your witness for him.'

I felt awed and thoughtful. I was certainly one of the weak things of the world. And yet God was going to use me! But how would he do it, I wondered.

Friends continued to encourage us in all sorts of ways as the tension mounted. Two new ones gave us a pretty black and white kitten, whom Mark named 'Pushka', meaning 'the gun' in Russian. She amused us all with her antics and was always good for a cuddle and a game.

The press continued to clamour for interviews and photographic sessions and I continued to refuse.

Then a man from a television company contacted Mr Bowden to suggest that it would be better for me to agree to one filming session than to have cameramen popping out of shops or running along beside me in the streets to get the pictures they wanted. My solicitor talked this over with me and in the end I agreed to a film session but still refused to give any interviews.

The amount of equipment and time involved in producing

this one short piece of film astonished me. The filming was to take place in the local park and to last half an hour or so. But first of all, there were preparations at my house. Then everything had to be set up in the park. Eventually, in public view, I had to walk along a prescribed line and smile! Afterwards, more time was taken up in seeing the film.

I found the whole experience a grim farce as well as a great strain. Although I had stated that I wouldn't give any interviews, I felt that I had to be on my guard against one or two people who, I sensed, were still hoping to get something in the way of 'copy' out of me.

I could, so I was told later, have asked for a fee or at least some reimbursement for my cooperation. At the time, my only thought was to get the business over with as quickly as possible so that we could be left in peace.

A man from a different television company called, the Sunday before the trial, but when requested to do so went away and, after a couple of phone calls, left me alone.

The weather grew bleak and blustery, and the huge dark cloud of the trial loomed closer. Just how close I had no idea.

17

Panic stations

Our house was a hive of activity. While I baked cakes and prepared soup, Craig and his grandpa were building a bonfire in the garden. Craig had wanted to celebrate November 5th and so I agreed that he could have one of his friends for the evening and invited my parents to come along, too. I wasn't feeling at all partyish and Mark and Steve weren't either, but we wanted Craig to have a good time.

By five o'clock preparations were well under way.

Then the telephone rang. The caller was Mr Davies, Geoff's solicitor.

'I'm afraid this is going to be rather a shock for you,' he said. 'The trial has been brought forward to Wednesday, November 10th.'

'But that's next week!' I exclaimed.

'I know,' Mr Davies responded. 'But the Director of Public Prosecutions telephoned to say that due to certain pressures, they had to bring the trial forward from November 29th.' I was still reeling, as he dropped the next bombshell: 'And the defence barrister, Mr Carman, wants to see you in London, on Monday.'

'Me! Why?'

'I don't know. But he definitely wants you there and said that all expenses incurred would be paid for.'

I suddenly thought about Geoff. How was he going to hear about this? Realising only too well how it would affect him, I said, 'I must go and see Geoff. I want to break the news to him myself.'

'I'll ring the prison and try to arrange a visit for you tomorrow,' he said. We talked briefly about where I could stay in London and Mr Davies promised to try and sort something out and contact me. Before ringing off, he gave me his home telephone number.

My mind was a whirl. Who would look after the boys while I was away? Would Jane still be able to come to the trial? What would I wear? The mail order firm hadn't yet sent the suit I'd ordered.

I passed on the news to my parents and the boys. Mum and dad immediately offered to help, and I asked whether they would have Craig to stay while I was away at the trial. They said they would, and nobly tried to continue with the bonfire party while I went to make some urgent phone calls.

I rang Jane to tell her the news. She couldn't manage, at such short notice, to have the Monday off, but said she would join me on the Tuesday and be with me at the trial on Wednesday. That was a relief. Then I telephoned Peter, who promised to have the boys the next day, Saturday, and agreed to Mark and Stephen staying with him during the time I would be away at the trial. Next there were friends and neighbours to contact, including Mr Glass, our minister, Mr Bowden, my solicitor, and Tim and Pam – a couple who had promised to put up, before the trial, a strong, wooden, lockable gate at the side of our house, to prevent the press and anyone else from getting into the back garden. The moment they heard of the changed situation they said they'd be round in the morning to do the job for us.

I rang off, very moved and thanking God for the wonderful friends he had given us.

Mr Davies telephoned with less encouraging news. The prison authorities had told him that a Saturday visit was out of the question: it wasn't my visiting day and I'd seen Geoff the previous day. Determinedly, I rang the West Mercia police to see whether they could do anything.

Some time later, they rang to tell me that they had managed to arrange an hour's visit for me the following day, adding that they couldn't on this occasion help with transport.

I went out to explain the latest development to my parents. Dad immediately said he would drive me to and from the prison and mum volunteered to go along too. I accepted both offers gratefully.

In between phone calls, I had been popping out into the garden to watch the fireworks and have something to eat. In spite of everything, the bonfire party had managed to proceed and Craig and his friend seemed to have enjoyed themselves.

After his friend had left and Craig had gone to bed, my parents and I discussed arrangements for a while and then they left and Mark, Stephen and I went to bed. I lay awake for some time, overwhelmed afresh at what had happened and all the repercussions from it.

The next morning, a large package arrived. My suit at last! I tried it on – and groaned. It was far too big as I'd lost even more weight. That meant two more things to do – return the suit or else I'd be charged for it, and somehow buy one that *did* fit.

I saw the boys off to Peter's for the day and prepared for the journey to Winson Green. We set off in wet and windy conditions, just as Pam and Tim arrived.

'I feel terrible about leaving you to work outdoors in this awful weather,' I told them, but they insisted that they'd be all right and cheerfully waved us off. As we drove along I kept thinking of how to break the news to Geoff.

My parents dropped me off at the prison. After the usual vetting procedures, I very apprehensively entered the visiting room.

One look at Geoff's distraught face, even before he blurted out, 'I know why you've come,' confirmed my fears. I hugged him – tears of sadness and frustration coming into my eyes – and then we sat down opposite to one another.

'How did you find out?' I asked.

'I read it in the paper a few moments ago,' he said angrily. 'After which the assistant governor came in, saw the paper and said, "Oh, dear, you've already seen it!" Or words to that effect.'

'I'm so sorry, Geoff,' I said. 'I did try to avoid something like that happening.'

'They won't tell me a thing!' my husband continued, bitterly. 'They must surely transfer me to London today so that I can meet Mr Carman.'

I had been told a little more than my husband had and saw no reason why he should be kept in the dark, so I said, 'I believe you're going to Brixton Prison on Monday and I think Mr Carman will see you there in the afternoon.'

'Monday!' he exploded, running his fingers agitatedly through his hair. 'What's the good of that? How can I possibly discuss the relevant details with him two days before my trial – not having previously *met* him even? I was told that we would have all the time we both needed before the trial . . .'

He continued to give vent to his frustration, anger and bewilderment.

Geoff spoke of Dr Marks, the psychiatrist. He'd had his second interview with him at Winson Green only the previous day. So how would he get a report through in time? What was it all about?

I had no answers – and could easily understand how the sudden change of plan, without any satisfactory explanation, had made him feel like a pawn in a very large political game.

'What do we do?' Geoff asked. 'We're nowhere near ready for the trial. We've got to get it put off.'

Could we do that, I wondered, then almost immediately decided that we probably couldn't or that it would prove pointless to do so. The whole thing seemed to have got out of hand and beyond our human control – but not, I still believed, beyond God's control.

To Geoff I said, 'I don't think that's going to be possible, Geoff. I think we're going to have to go through with it.'

Geoff continued to protest, his agitation increasing, until the hour was up and we had to say goodbye and part. I felt wretched at having to leave him in the state he was in.

The drive home was a gloomy one. I cried a good deal, and my parents, realising I must have had a traumatic meeting, tactfully refrained from questioning me about it.

At Tewkesbury, hoping the diversion would help, dad took us out to lunch. Afterwards mum suggested a look around the shops to find me a suit. It was a kind thought, so, although I wasn't in the mood for clothes buying, I went to a few shops. But nothing fitted, or looked right, so we drove on.

My parents dropped me at Laburnham Cottage before driving to their home. I had some essential shopping to do, and forced myself to go into town to do it. I had just finished when I remembered the suit. I looked at my watch. It was five o'clock already! Quickly I walked along the promenade to a store which had a sale on. A light grey suit caught my eye. It had been reduced to thirty pounds, which was all the money I had left in the bank. I tried it on.

'A perfect fit,' said the assistant. She was right. As I paid the money I was praying, 'Lord, I'm buying this in faith. Please meet our needs and help me to honour you when I wear this suit.'

I left the shop just before closing time and returned home to find someone enquiring about Geoff's squash racquet which I'd been advertising for sale in the local paper. She bought this.

Later someone called and bought the car radio which I'd also advertised.

The proceeds from selling these two items came to thirty pounds.

Thank you, Lord! was my immediate reaction. What had happened was a lovely welcome reminder that although everything seemed chaotic, God knew about it all and was in control – even of the details.

18

Hurried preparations

After the evening meal, Mr Glass came round to talk and pray with us.

'Mr Carman wants to see me and I keep wondering why,' I told him. 'If he does by any chance ask me to speak at the trial, what shall I do? Or say? Have you any advice for me?' He looked thoughtful then said, 'Don't say too much. Don't lay your life on the line.'

'I'll try not to,' I answered.

'On the day you will know what to say,' he continued. 'And we'll be praying for you. As a pastor, I believe I'm responsible for my congregation, so whatever happens in the future I'll be ready to help and support you.'

Very touched, I thanked him.

Craig wandered in. Mr Glass drew him in quite naturally and then talked helpfully to him about the trial – trying to reassure him over my having to go to it – and afterwards prayed with him.

When Craig had gone we continued to talk for a while.

'Would you mind if I tell the congregation about the change of date and ask for their support and continuing prayers? Or would that upset Craig?' he asked.

'No – he'd like that and so would I.'

When Mr Glass left, Craig went to bed in the room which he and Stephen shared with some gerbils which Geoff and I had given them one Christmas. As I said goodnight to him I tried to make sure he understood and was happy about what had been arranged.

'Grandma and grandpa will take care of you while I'm away,' I told him. 'And they'll decide with you whether it's best for you to stay at home or go to school next week. I'm sure you'll be all right, whatever happens, and I'll be back soon.'

Later I talked to Stephen and Mark about what would be happening as far as they were concerned. They showed their feelings less obviously than Craig, but I sensed that they were apprehensive and tense, too.

Sunday was a hectic day of packing and making preparations. We had lunch with mum and dad. The meal over, the boys went and amused themselves while we tried to finalise my plans. I rang Mr Bowden to find out whether he'd managed to do anything about accommodation.

'Yes,' he replied, sounding pleased. 'A friend of ours, a Christian barrister, has offered us a flat at the Oval for Tuesday night. So the three of us who are going to be with you at the trial, can stay there and go to the Central Criminal Court together on Wednesday.'

'That's great – and really kind of your friend,' I said. I took down the address of the flat and we arranged that Jane and I should meet him and Mr Hirst there at about eight-thirty on Tuesday evening.

'I'll ring Mr Davies and see whether he's got any ideas for Monday night,' I said.

'If you stay at a hotel, you should go under a pseudonym,' Mr Bowden said.

'That's a point! What shall I go as? Mrs Brown? Mrs White?' I said, with a laugh.

'Too obvious. How about Mrs Jackson?'

'All right. But what about a Christian name? I know! I could use my middle name – Marjorie.'

'Fine. Mrs Marjorie Jackson. And Jane will need a pseudonym too.'

I rang off and told my parents what had happened. It was something to laugh about and share lightheartedly with the boys.

Next I telephoned Mr Davies to bring him up to date. He

gave me the name of the hotel he'd be staying at, adding, 'Why don't you book in there for Monday night?'

'All right,' I said.

'Would you like a lift up to London with me tomorrow?'

'Thanks very much, but dad has offered to take me,' I said. We arranged to meet in the foyer of the hotel on Monday lunchtime.

Dad offered to make the next phone call. Mum and I watched him dial the number of the hotel. Then, after a pause, he said, 'I'd like to book a single room for bed and breakfast for Monday, November 8th. The name is Mrs Marjorie Jackson.' With only a few seconds' hesitation, he continued, 'Thirty-six, Pecked Lane, Tewkesbury, Gloucestershire.'

He put the phone down and we burst out laughing.

'I forgot about the address,' I said. 'Well done!'

'Did it sound very false?' he asked, with a smile.

'Not at all. You made it sound most realistic,' I said.

Later the boys were amused to hear how their grandfather had risen to the occasion. We all needed such rare moments of light relief.

Jane, whom I rang next, entered into the spirit of the thing immediately and plumped for the name 'Mrs Edwards'.

Further phone calls had to be made to Mr Davies and Mr Bowden to tell them of my 'address' and Jane's pseudonym.

I had to be home by four o'clock as Dr Marks had arranged to come and see me. I'd never met a psychiatrist before and wondered what he'd be like. His report assessing Geoff's personality and problems had struck me, when I'd read it, as very perceptive.

He arrived on time: a younger-middle-aged man; tall, slim and quietly spoken, with dark hair and a rather serious expression.

I quickly felt at ease with him as we talked about Geoff and he made notes on my comments.

'Can he be treated and helped?' I asked.

'Well, it would be easier if he were out of prison, but we could certainly try,' he answered. 'Already things are better through all this being brought out into the open. It's when people hide away with no one to talk to about their problems that they can't cope and are completely overwhelmed by them.'

That made sense. Dr Marks continued, 'Geoff strikes me as a sad, introverted person, but because of the hope which his relationship with you has given him, and the possibility of help, I'm sure his future could be brighter than his past.'

I felt somewhat cheered. Here at last was someone saying positive, hopeful things about Geoff.

Craig, to whom I had already explained who Dr Marks was, came into the lounge.

'How do you feel about Geoff?' Dr Marks asked him gently.

Craig's face grew sad as he said, 'He's a great dad and I miss him a lot.'

Dr Marks caught my eye and smiled.

'Out of the mouths of children . . .' he quoted softly. 'What more can I say after that? That speaks volumes to me. And it's a good point at which to end our meeting, don't you think?'

'Yes,' I agreed, with a catch in my throat.

'I'll do my best to get my report to London by Tuesday,' he said as he rose to leave. 'But I still have a lot of work to do on it and the pressure will be considerable.'

After he had left I prepared a tea of sorts which we all ate in the kitchen. Then Craig and I went to Elim.

It was a good service. At the end, as the congregation stood for the final blessing, Mr Glass said, 'We would, as a church, like to assure Mrs Prime and her family of our continued prayers and support in the coming weeks, and particularly on Wednesday, November 10th. Her husband's trial has been unexpectedly brought forward and will now take place on that day. Let's now commit this family to God.'

He prayed, and the congregation said a resounding 'Amen'. A sense of quietness and peace filled me. It was a feeling that was never completely swamped or pushed out in the coming days.

After the service friends crowded round to show their care and to promise help and prayer.

Back home there was still much to be done. I made arrangements for the cat and the gerbils to be looked after, did the ironing and packing and told the neighbours of our possible movements as well as warning them about what the press might do.

At last I fell into bed, physically exhausted but so strung up emotionally that it was a long time before sleep brought a few hours' relief and forgetfulness.

19

Questions

'It looks like the end of the world,' I said, peering up through the windscreen at the dark awe-inspiring sky. Rain and hail were pounding down, making our progress slow, if not at times almost impossible.

It was just after ten o'clock in the morning and dad and I were on our way to London for the long-dreaded trial, now only two days away. The press had been lying in wait near the house, but we'd managed to take avoiding action, thanks to keen-eyed Mark who'd spotted them on his journey to school and had doubled back to warn us.

Already I felt exhausted. After getting up early I'd had to finalise all the arrangements and do the last-minute packing as well as seeing Mark and Stephen off to school on their bikes. Their courage in trying to carry on as usual was remarkable.

Then a very upset Craig had had to go. He remembers vividly my saying to him, 'Don't forget, whatever happens Jesus really loves and cares for you,' and then dad's arrival and his words: 'Always remember we really love you, Craig.'

Afterwards, the two had gone off in dad's car, but on the way, as if to illustrate the principle that it never rains but it pours, they'd run out of petrol, and dad had had to sort that out in addition to everything else he'd had to do before driving me to London.

Meanwhile, I'd had to dash to the post office to send back the ill-fitting suit, and then hurry home to wash my hair, ring the driving school to cancel my test – booked, ironically, for the new date of the trial – and read my post.

There had been two loving, supportive letters – one from mum and the other from a friend, who'd urged me to read Psalm 31, and had also written out a rhyme.

His presence and hand-hold we often don't feel,
Although we may wish that we could,
But we know from his word he is with us unseen,
And silently plans for our good.

Not the sort of composition likely to win any literary prizes, yet God had spoken to me as I'd read it. In the midst of all my rushing about, it had been a reminder that God was planning good things even when the opposite appeared to be happening.

Now, sitting in the passenger seat of dad's car, I tried to unwind a little as our seemingly frail vehicle battled its way through the thunderstorm. We stopped once for a drink and a break, but after that, we kept going until we reached our destination.

It was a relief to arrive and take refuge in the carpeted and cushioned comfort of the hotel. While dad parked the car, I walked to the reception desk and, with as much panache as I could muster, announced myself as Mrs Marjorie Jackson. The receptionist handed me a key and I went in search of my room.

This place spelt elegance and luxury to me and as I approached my room, I visualised the dream bedroom on the other side of the door. A moment later I stepped inside – only to face instant disillusionment.

The room was poky and dark with sparse, unattractive furnishings. I felt keen disappointment and then, remembering the cost of one night's stay in this room, indignation. But far more pressing matters were soon occupying my thoughts.

I would be seeing Mr Carman after lunch and felt totally unprepared for such a meeting. He was bound to ask me about Geoff.

I found a pad and Biro and sat down on the bed to try and collect my thoughts. Memories from the past five years came crowding into my mind and I started to jot down comments about Geoff – as husband, father figure and breadwinner; as a person in his own right, with strong political convictions and deep personal problems . . .

My father's entrance interrupted my train of thought. I put my notebook and pen aside to listen as he gave an account of his parking problems.

Soon afterwards, Mr Davies arrived. When he'd laid claim to his room, the three of us met in the foyer and proceeded to the carvery where we ordered a Welsh rarebit apiece, with a cup of tea for me and a glass of beer for each of the men.

As we ate and talked, my thoughts kept turning to the coming meeting with Geoff's barrister. I knew he was an eminent QC and that he'd defended Jeremy Thorpe, but that was about all. What would he be like? What would he want to know?

When it was time to leave, dad said he would rather stay behind and returned to my room while Mr Davies and I went out and hailed a taxi. Our destination was the Temple or Inns of Court, lying somewhere between Fleet Street and the Embankment. I knew that these were the barristers' chambers but, never having had anything to do with barristers or their chambers, I didn't know what to expect and felt rather nervous.

We were driven skilfully through the crowded London streets and deposited at the Temple. This turned out to be a huge complex of enclosed buildings. The moment I set foot in the precincts, I could imagine myself back in the world of Charles Dickens.

We crossed cobbled courtyards and walked along narrow, arched passageways between brick buildings.

Entering one of these, we were greeted courteously by a young man who introduced himself as Mr Clover. He was, he said, the junior barrister called in at short notice to replace the one originally designated to assist Mr Carman but unable to do so now that the date of the trial had been changed.

I liked Mr Clover's open friendly manner. He led us up steep stone steps. I looked at the worn treads and wondered briefly how many famous feet had walked this way before us. At the top of each short flight, corridors led off in different directions. The place struck me as being rather like a rabbit warren.

Mr Carman's suite of rooms lay at the end of a short passage about three storeys up. Mr Clover admitted us, then showed us into a spacious, beautifully proportioned room. Panelled walls and a high ornamental ceiling gave the place touches of old-world elegance, I thought. I noticed, too, a large number of leather-bound volumes on the bookshelves, several leather easy chairs and two desks – the larger being nearer the windows and the other opposite.

'I'm sorry Mr Carman isn't here yet, but do sit down,' Mr Clover said. Mr Davies and I sat facing the big desk and Mr Clover nearby. After a few moments' conversation, the door suddenly burst open and a shortish gentleman hurried in exclaiming, 'Good afternoon! Good afternoon! Sorry to keep you waiting.'

He dispensed hurriedly with the introductions, then, having shed his coat, seated himself behind the larger desk and looked shrewdly at me from behind owlish spectacles.

Sensing that I was in the presence of a powerful personality, and one that appeared to be feeling somewhat tense just then, I became even more apprehensive. The questions which he proceeded to ask me, and his rather direct manner, did nothing to calm me down. After establishing who I was and how long Geoff and I had been married, he asked, 'What are your political views, Mrs Prime?'

I managed to say something about believing in socialism as an ideal but realising that it only worked in an ideal world, which ours wasn't and never would be.

'Do you have any communist leanings?'

That was easier to answer.

'None whatsoever. I dislike all political extremes either to the right or the left.'

'What led you to tell the authorities about your husband's spying activities?'

Here we go, I thought, sending up a quick prayer and taking a deep breath.

'I'm a Christian,' I said. 'And that's why I had to do what I did. I couldn't ignore my conscience nor can I desert my husband. I want to stand by him and also tell the truth. He's not the man he is made out to be . . .'

As I talked about Geoff and our situation I sensed a change in Mr Carman. His expression conveyed interest and when he next spoke his tone seemed more sympathetic.

'Were you shocked to realise how serious the situation was?'

'Yes – but I haven't yet been given a clear idea as to what Geoff is supposed to have done and what it all means.'

'I shall know more tomorrow after I've been in touch with the Security Services,' he told me.

Talk about the eleventh hour! I thought. Then he added, 'But it does seem serious.' This was a comment too devastating to dwell on, so I hastened to pursue a different topic. Why, I wanted to know, had the trial been brought forward – so causing acute distress or inconvenience, or both, for those personally and professionally involved?

He replied, 'The Director of Public Prosecutions wants to bring the date of the trial forward because of administrative problems and possible leaks to the press later in the week.'

'What sort of leaks?'

'I don't know. But I think you'll understand later why the date was changed and see that it was better for your husband this way. All I can say is that it is felt that the leaks are likely to make things look more damaging for him.'

Though mystified, I accepted this.

Now as I write the book I'm still none the wiser.

Then came the question, 'Mrs Prime, would you be willing to stand up in court and say publicly what you have been telling me privately about your husband?'

My usual reaction on being asked to do anything in public

is an emphatic, 'No.' Instead, I answered, promptly, 'Yes, I will.'

All along, underneath my nervousness and fear, I had been aware that God was in control and the moment the question had been asked, I'd felt suddenly sure of the answer he wanted me to give.

'You don't have to do this,' Mr Carman said.

'I know, but I think I should and I believe it's right,' I replied.

Tea was brought in and he invited me to be 'mother'. I complied shakily, terrified of dropping the handsome teapot and smashing the bone china cups or slopping tea on to the polished table or plush carpet. Somehow these catastrophes were avoided.

Over tea the conversation became more general and then Mr Carman suddenly observed, 'Mrs Prime, I think you're a likeable, intelligent woman and I admire you.'

Surprised and embarrassed by this flattering remark, I quickly changed the subject.

20

Turmoil

At about quarter to four, Mr Carman suggested we should go and see Geoff at Brixton.

'Could I ring and let my father know what is happening?' I asked.

'Be my guest,' he invited, indicating a very modern telephone on the leather-topped desk. Hesitantly I pressed various buttons and eventually succeeded, with Mr Davies' help, in getting through to my father.

'We're off to see Geoff and I don't think we'll be back for some time,' I told him.

'Then I think I'll drive home, if it's all right by you,' he said. 'You won't need me any more, will you?'

'No, I won't – thank you,' I said.

After I'd put the phone down, Mr Clover picked it up again to ring Brixton prison. He explained that he and Mr Carman needed to see their client Mr Geoffrey Prime. There was a pause, after which Mr Clover said, 'Just a moment, please,' and then, putting his hand over the mouthpiece, addressed Mr Carman with the words, 'They say it can't be arranged at such short notice.'

Looking purposeful, Mr Carman held out his hand for the phone. When it was given to him, he spoke crisply into it, informing the person at the other end that the Director of Public Prosecutions had assured him that he could have access to his client at any time of day or night and he fully intended to see him that afternoon.

This message had to be repeated more than once, to one

prison official after another, before it had the desired effect. Eventually, permission granted, the four of us left the Temple by taxi and were soon speeding towards Brixton. Mr Carman, briefcase in hand, sat opposite me and asked questions with an air of genuine interest and concern. How was I coping? What effect was all this having on my family – the boys in particular? I found myself able to talk freely.

'Has the press been bothering you?' he asked.

I answered with feeling.

'What sort of sums are they offering for your story?'

'Anything up to or even over £100,000.'

We were passing through depressing surroundings. Everywhere there was evidence of poverty and neglect.

The taxi turned into a narrow road and after a few moments pulled up in front of a solid metal bar across the road, operated by a man in a cubicle to one side. Mr Carman opened the glass partition to speak to the taxi driver. He explained who we were, adding, 'We're in a terrible hurry, so please speak to the official then drive us to the main gates.'

'Sorry, guv'nor, it's against regulations,' said the driver. 'You'll have to walk the rest of the way.' Protesting strenuously, Mr Carman climbed out of the taxi and we followed suit. He spoke to the man in the cubicle, then we all walked, in fine driving rain, down a long path adjacent to the prison walls, which were massive and topped by coils of barbed wire.

After the usual checks, we were admitted past large solid-looking doors into the reception area – where it became even more apparent that this was not Mr Carman's day. Barking furiously, a guard dog on a long chain went for his leg. Almost immediately the animal was brought to heel by its prison officer owner and profuse apologies were offered, but our visit had hardly got off to a good start.

I was abruptly sobered, a moment later, by seeing what looked to me like bullet holes in the glass of one of the windows. Later I was told that I had been mistaken about this, but at the time the sight served as a forcible reminder of the realities of prison life and therefore of Geoff's life. At times, stimulating activities or contacts with people made it possible to push to one side the grim facts of our situation. But it was never very long before something would occur to ensure that they occupied the centre of my thoughts again.

After clearance we were all taken to a small room. There I was left alone, and glad to be so, while the three men went off to see Geoff. All I had with me were my New Testament and a booklet commenting on one of the books in it – 2 Corinthians. The time was about twenty minutes past four.

I opened the booklet and started to read it. The comments were all about Paul's sufferings but utterly relevant to mine. I drank in every word, looking up the verses in the Bible and crying out to God to help me as he had helped Paul long ago.

Tea was brought in twice, but otherwise I read and prayed uninterruptedly for about two hours. It was a sorely needed oasis.

Meanwhile, as I was to learn later, Geoff was being given some devastating news. For the first time, and with the trial only two days away, he was learning that he faced seven charges under Section 1 of the Official Secrets Act. Up till that moment he had been hoping that his full statement would have had a bearing on the number of charges made against him.

Unaware of all this, I continued to read and pray until a prison officer came in and said, 'Would you come with me, please?' I followed him downstairs, along several corridors and past several doors and gates, before meeting an anxious-looking Mr Clover.

'Your husband's in a bad way and we're not making much progress,' he told me. 'Could you please go in and try to calm him down? Every time we mention your name he gets dreadfully upset.'

My spirits plummeted. It was all just as I'd feared. With a heavy heart I went into the room indicated by Mr Clover. Geoff, pacing up and down like a caged animal, turned a completely distraught face towards me.

'We'll give you a moment or two alone,' Mr Carman said, and he and the other two men left the room.

I went to Geoff, put my arms round him and kissed him. There was tension in every line of his body. After a moment, we sat down.

'They can't do this to us!' he burst out. 'How can we have a proper trial at such short notice? The whole thing's a mess! Today they drove me all the way from Winson Green to this place with shrieking sirens. I only arrived here about two hours ago. It's too absurd for words! I haven't slept, I can't think straight and the pressure on all of us is just too great.'

'I know,' I said. 'But let's talk to Mr Carman and the others and try to get something sorted out.' Geoff continued to express his totally understandable anger and frustration and I failed to calm him down. Rather, as I listened to him, doubts started to disturb me.

Was I deluded in thinking we were in God's hands? Were we nothing more than pawns in a political game? Would justice truly be fair and impartial or would my husband be made a scapegoat?

The men returned and Geoff's face resumed its hostile expression.

'We need to carry on going through your statement,' Mr Carman said.

'In that case, is it right that my wife should be here?' Geoff asked.

Mr Carman replied, 'I had a long talk with your wife this afternoon and she has agreed to speak in court on your behalf.'

Geoff's face registered amazement, as he turned to me and asked, 'Are you sure you want to do this, Rhona? Do you understand what it means? Is it right for you to do it?'

'If it'll help you in any way, of course I'll do it,' I told him. I thought I saw his expression lighten just a little.

Skilfully, doggedly, Mr Carman went on working through the statement, plying Geoff with cigarettes as he did so, while I held my husband's hand and prayed silently.

Later a warder brought in on a tray a plate piled high with starchy-looking food. Geoff left it largely untouched.

The difficult interview proceeded.

'How on earth can the psychiatric report be ready in time?' Geoff wanted to know. 'Dr Marks only finished interviewing me on Friday.'

'I have given instructions for his report to be delivered to my chambers on Tuesday,' Mr Carman said.

At about eight o'clock, when Mr Carman decided to call it a day, Geoff was being only marginally more cooperative than he had been at first.

A sleeping draught was brought in and the three men got up and made for the door. On the way Mr Carman spoke in an aside to me.

'Please try to persuade him to take the sleeping draught. It's vital that he should have a good night's sleep. He looks terrible – completely worn out.'

'Of course he does, with all this totally unexpected and intolerable pressure,' I retorted.

Alone together, Geoff and I said our goodbyes.

'Do you really think we should go through with this?' he asked in a tone of weary despair. 'It doesn't seem right to let them push us around like this.'

'I agree, my dear,' I said. 'But I just don't think we have any option. Mr Davies doesn't think so anyway. And even if we did manage to get the trial postponed, we might be no better off. They might even hold that against us.'

'I suppose you're right,' he said, dejectedly.

'You've had a terrible day, Geoff, and you must get some sleep. Please take the sleeping draught.'

Geoff picked up the little glass and drank its contents.

Mr Carman reappeared to say, 'We must go now. But your wife can visit you tomorrow morning for a while and then Mr Davies will see you to answer questions regarding anything that's worrying you.'

Anything! I thought wryly.

It was agony walking away from Geoff in the state that he was in, but it had to be done.

21

Build-up

We were whisked by taxi away from the depressing dinginess of Brixton and towards London's West End. Mr Clover had another engagement and was dropped off at a suitable spot but the rest of us alighted at a large hotel. In the elegance of this place Mr Davies and I were treated to drinks by Mr Carman. As I sipped mine he said, 'Your husband is in a bad way and still very aggressive.'

'I know,' I said. 'You're seeing him in the worst possible light, which is hardly surprising. He's not the sort of person to be able to cope with a mad rush, and who would, anyway? It's so unfair . . .'

Mr Carman listened, asking questions now and then, as I continued to talk about Geoff and our situation.

'I've dealt with a variety of cases,' he said, afterwards, 'but never one like this. It's stranger than fiction. I find it almost unbelievable and I'm sure you must feel the same at times.'

'I certainly do,' I assured him. Mr Davies joined in and our three-way conversation went on for a time. Then Mr Carman left by taxi and Mr Davies and I walked back to our hotel.

Once there, I went straight up to my room. I unpacked, then rang my parents to tell them what I had decided to do. They received the news quietly but I realised afresh how hard all this was on them.

After the phone call, far too strung up to sleep, I took a book and went downstairs into the pizzeria. There I ordered lasagne and gateau with wine, followed by coffee. In other circumstances I would have revelled in the unaccustomed luxury, the service and the food. As it was, the situation seemed unreal and I kept thinking of Geoff alone in his bleak prison cell. The transition from Brixton to this luxury hotel had been too abrupt, the contrast too stark. The person sitting in plush surroundings wining and dining herself wasn't me. It was Mrs Marjorie Jackson. While she ate and drank, I felt utterly alone and desperately sad, surrounded as I was by happy, chattering people – each belonging to a partner or included in a close-knit group. Hardest to bear was the sight of doting, dewy-eyed newly-wed or newly-engaged couples. I did not grudge them their happiness but it emphasised poignantly my own situation.

I forced myself to eat a little, while pretending to concentrate on my book but unable to take in a single line.

It was past midnight before I returned to my room to undress and get into bed. I had escaped the happy diners only to be confronted by my own fearful, accusing thoughts.

Whatever happened to Geoff on Wednesday, I would have brought it on him by going to the authorities. If they gave him twenty-five years, I thought, I couldn't bear it. It reassured me to think of Geoff's defence counsel. Mr Carman and Mr Clover struck me as being extremely able, and very human, as well. I had to agree with some of Geoff's criticisms of our country, but it was certainly a blessing that through legal aid we could have the services of top professionals like these.

I remembered my friend's letter and opened my Bible to Psalm 31. It might have been written for me. The writer's troubled thoughts reflected mine and his prayers became mine.

God was with me. The minister, some of my family, the church members and many others would be praying for me. Reminded of this, I revived a little.

Suddenly I remembered the verses which Paul Snow had given to me and thought, *Perhaps it's at the trial that God wants me, somehow, to be a light and witness for him.*

I woke early after a restless night. A bath refreshed me a

little and then I went down to the carvery. All around me people were eating typically English breakfasts, so I helped myself to one. By the time I'd sat down, I was feeling too sick to enjoy it, but managed to swallow just a few mouthfuls.

Then it was time to visit Geoff. I remembered that Jane would be arriving some time in the morning and went to the reception desk to leave a message for her.

'If a Mrs Edwards calls, please tell her that Mrs Jackson has had to go out and ask her to wait in my room or in the foyer,' I said.

The receptionist made a note of my message and I left the hotel and took a taxi to Brixton. At the prison, as well as having to go through the usual checking procedures, I was frisked before being allowed to see Geoff.

He was in a different room, and looking, I noticed with relief, much calmer.

'I thought about tossing a coin to see whether we should go along with this trial tomorrow or not,' he said. I laughed and he responded with a smile and the words, 'But that's not the way to do things, is it?'

'No,' I agreed. 'God doesn't work like that.'

We talked about the trial. Clearly he was trying to come to terms with what now seemed inevitable.

When Mr Davies arrived Geoff had some questions for him and the two men talked.

A warder brought in Geoff's dinner. It looked like the worst sort of school meal and after a few moments he pushed it to one side.

It was after one by the time Mr Davies and I left. Back in the hotel my spirits rose at the sight of Jane waiting for me.

She and I lunched with Mr Davies and then the two of us walked along the street talking, until it was time for me to set off for the Temple. Jane said she'd window-shop while I was away.

Mr Carman greeted Mr Davies and me courteously. Once again tea was served and I was asked to dispense it from a large elegant teapot. As we were drinking, Mr Carman said, 'I've just been with the Security Services people to discover how damaging they consider your husband's espionage activities to have been.' My heart skipped a beat at these words and then the familiar feeling of dread was back in full force as he continued, 'I'm afraid things don't look good. According to the people there the situation is grave.'

Teacup in hand, I tried to grapple with my feelings as he went on, 'All I can suggest is that you urge your husband to continue to cooperate fully with the Security Services after the trial. This could help when it comes to the matter of his parole.'

He started talking about the trial and the sort of questions he would be asking me. Somehow I had to turn my mind to thinking about answers.

Later Mr Davies got ready to go to Brixton Prison, bearing various messages from Mr Carman, and one from me, to Geoff.

'Please ask him from me to agree to cooperate with the authorities and to take his sleeping draught this evening,' I said, adding, 'Oh, yes, and ask him if he would please read Psalm 31.'

Mr Davies noted this down, making no comment, then left. I returned to the hotel, beginning to feel very unsure of myself and to have doubts about the rightness of my decision.

Knowing that I could bank on receiving an honest answer from Jane, I talked the matter over with her when we met at the hotel.

'Do you think it's right – my agreeing to be a witness?' I asked.

'Yes, I do,' she said, sounding reassuringly emphatic.

We went to the carvery for a meal: steak, cheesecake and coffee. Being with a friend made all the difference, particularly when, as happened at times, waves of panic washed over me as I thought about the next day.

I phoned my parents to find out how they and the boys were and to bring them up to date, and Jane phoned her family.

In the evening we took a taxi to the Oval and met up with Mr Hirst and Mr Bowden as arranged. Being in a home rather than in an hotel, and among supportive Christians, was the best possible situation for me that evening. The kindness of those who had offered us the flat and of my three companions touched me deeply.

Mr Davies rang to say that he'd been to see Geoff and that he'd been much calmer and had agreed to all the requests. Mr Carman and Mr Clover, he said, would be seeing my husband again just before the trial.

I spent some of the evening in my room, reading my Bible and praying, often tearfully.

I kept asking God to give me his grace and strength and use me in whatever way he wanted to on the next day.

And be with Geoff, I added. *May he read and be helped by that psalm . . .*

Feeling strangely peaceful, I fell asleep.

22

Trial

'Geoffrey Arthur Prime, you are charged on two indict-
ments,' the Clerk of the Court was saying in slow, solemn
tones. 'The first indictment consists of seven counts. In the
first count you are charged . . .'

I listened, in frozen horror mixed with incredulity. Was I
really here, in the highest court in the land, hearing my
husband indicted for sexual offences and espionage, I wondered bemusedly, while being only too aware of the realities
of the situation.

All around me were legal dignitaries, members of the
police and Social Services and representatives of the media.
Mr Davies sat beside me, but Jane, Mr Bowden and Mr
Hirst were behind me – out of sight somewhere in the gallery. Below were Mr Carman and Mr Clover and their
opposite members, gowned and wigged, and above and to
my right, in full regalia, sat the Lord Chief Justice.

And then there was Geoff – a heartrending sight, as he
stood in the dock, on the same level as the judge but to my
left, handcuffed to two guards and looking haggard. He was
wearing his own dark blue suit over a blue-and-white striped
shirt and a blue tie.

On and on went the voice of the Clerk of the Court as he
read out the seven counts of the first indictment and the three
counts of the second.

So much had happened since half-past five that morning.
Jane and I had spent an hour reading the Bible, praying and
worshipping together and then Mr Hirst had presided at a

simple intensely moving communion service for the four of us.

Breakfast had followed and afterwards, clutching coats and umbrellas on account of the grey skies, we'd walked to the tube and squeezed on to a train; I all the while feeling very conspicuous in my hat – an item of clothing which, contrary to my expectations, no one else had seemed to be wearing.

Coming out of the Bank tube station, we'd headed towards a back entrance to the Old Bailey.

At a greengrocer's, Mr Hirst and Mr Bowden had stopped to check on the time, while Jane and I had waited outside.

'All the best,' someone had shouted. We'd spun round to see a television reporter whom I'd met before – emerging briefly from a taxi to greet me, wave and smile before driving off again. Thanks to his tip-off – for which he later apologised – on coming within sight of the building we'd been confronted by a scene that had made me go weak at the knees: a large body of press people straight ahead and hovering round the entrances through one of which we'd hoped to slip unobtrusively inside.

Mr Hirst and Mr Bowden had reacted promptly, by walking directly in front of us and Jane had grabbed my arm and said, 'Keep your head down and count the stripes on Mr Bowden's trousers.' That had forced a smile out of me as I'd pulled my hat down and tried hard to focus on my solicitor's pin-stripes, while newsmen had surged round – almost knocking us over at one point. Closer and closer they'd pressed, taking photographs or firing inane questions – 'How are you, Mrs Prime?' 'How do you feel?'

I'd felt terrible – all peace and assurance gone and replaced by fear and tension. A moment later I'd been almost overcome by faintness and had had to lean heavily on Jane. She'd just managed to push me inside via the revolving door before I'd passed right out.

On coming round, I'd been aware that all sense of strain had gone and the feeling of peace was back.

'Who is this lady?' an official had asked those near me and on being answered had said, 'Come this way.' Jane and others helping me, we'd crossed the passage to get further away from the entrance. There, still very wobbly, I'd sat down. Someone had brought water and I'd sipped it.

Feeling stronger, I'd been taken up some stairs and along a passage into a large airy room. Too dazed to take in much, I'd nevertheless been aware of beautifully carved woodwork, domed ceilings and marble floors along the way.

Once in the room, surrounded by kind friends and helpful officials, I'd recovered my strength.

When the time had come for the trial to commence, Jane, Mr Hirst and Mr Bowden had had to go to the gallery while Mr Davies and I had been shown into some seats in the main body of the courtroom.

And here I was, listening, for the tenth and last time, to the Clerk of the Court asking, 'Are you guilty or not guilty?' and my husband's response: 'Guilty'.

Then the Attorney General, Sir Michael Havers QC, rose to his feet and opened for the prosecution, dealing first with the three offences on the second indictment.

As he spoke I remembered the dreadful interview during which Geoff had admitted in my hearing to two sexual offences and had afterwards (so I'd learnt later) confessed to a third and, while on the way to the police station, pointed out where this had taken place. Hearing the details all over again was sheer torture.

At last the Attorney General moved on to the first indictment – that of espionage. Still struggling with the emotions aroused by the other indictment I was aware that he was giving brief details of my husband's career.

Born in Stoke on Trent and educated in Staffordshire, Geoff had joined the RAF in 1956. After serving in Africa and completing a Russian language course he had been posted in 1964 to RAF Gatow in West Berlin where his work had been of a classified nature. After his discharge from the RAF in 1968, having been vetted and given clearance, he'd worked with the Government Services in London until 1976 when he'd moved to Cheltenham to work at GCHQ until his resignation in 1977.

Sir Michael then gave an account of the interrogation by the police of Geoff, culminating in his full confession and statement. He proceeded to turn to some of the salient features of that statement.

He spoke of how Geoff had become involved in espionage and been trained and equipped by the Russians, and referred to secret writing, coded radio transmissions, microdots, dead letterbox procedure, one-time pads and a codename, password and miniature camera. I thought about the disruption which the search for the last-named object had caused in our home. Geoff had told me that the only place other than the loft where he used to keep it, was the boot of his taxi. However, despite extensive searches, its whereabouts remained a mystery to us all.

The Attorney General was giving details of the seven counts. It seemed that on six occasions, Geoff had had meetings with his Soviet contacts or left material for them in various places. The remaining count, which the Clerk of the Court had called the second one, related to information transmitted through letters and similar means throughout the period.

Listening, I was struck afresh by the tragic irony of the fact that though the bulk of Geoff's espionage activities – five out of the seven counts – had taken place prior to our marriage, it was my action in going to the police that had begun the chain of events leading to the trial . . .

The judge was calling for an adjournment so that secret material relating to what Geoff had disclosed or passed on could be revealed *in camera*. Very few people were permitted to be present at these proceedings and the rest of us dispersed. I was taken to a nearby room and, to my great relief, left alone there.

With shaking hands and crying out again to God for help, I took my New Testament from my handbag and opened it. My eyes fell on the words: 'You sympathised with those in prison and joyfully accepted the confiscation of your property because you knew that you yourselves had better and lasting possessions. So do not throw away your confidence; it will be richly rewarded. You need to persevere so that when you have done the will of God, you will receive what he has promised.'

I was filled with elation. Out of the whole New Testament, I had opened at a passage that mentioned prison and the confiscation of property – both of which were significant topics to me! Eagerly, I reread the words and scanned the verses before and after them – becoming increasingly convinced that God was saying to me, *Don't give up. Keep doing what you believe to be right. To be stripped is painful but necessary. Your hands must be empty. I am the true judge and I will keep my promises.*

Fresh hope and courage flowed into me.

Mr Carman's clerk came in to see whether I was lonely and needed company. I wasn't and didn't, but I appreciated the thoughtfulness while feeling thankful that he hadn't arrived earlier. We talked for a while about school meals: a topic which I'm sure interested neither of us just then.

The adjournment, having lasted about forty minutes, ended, and I was taken back into the courtroom.

The court reassembled and Mr Carman rose to speak on Geoff's behalf. His client, he said, particularly wished him to emphasise that he had not involved anyone in the West in his espionage and that, having confessed, he was anxious to cooperate with the authorities in future interviews and to give them any further information he could in order to help repair some of the damage he had caused. Referring to the sexual offences, the QC added, 'A matter of private concern but of no less importance in Your Lordship's court, is the utter shame and profound remorse that he would wish me to express to the children concerned and their parents.'

'What kind of a man is Geoffrey Prime?' Mr Carman then asked, and proceeded to answer the question by saying that he was a loner and someone who felt inadequate and at odds with society.

As he went on to mention some of the circumstances of

Geoff's unhappy childhood I glanced at my husband, knowing what torture this exposure of very personal matters would be for him. His face was a careful mask but his bearing, I felt, conveyed his sense of humiliation.

My heart went out to him. Others too, I believed, after hearing what had just been said, would be feeling some degree of understanding or sympathy for the man in the dock.

'But he is forty-four!' interposed the Lord Chief Justice, dashing my hopes. Evidently he – the person whose opinion counted most in this situation – considered such matters irrelevant to the proceedings.

In reply, Mr Carman suggested that Geoff's childhood experiences, while not excusing his present conduct, could be helpful in arriving at an understanding of the man, and of how, at the age of thirty when stationed in West Berlin with the RAF, his loneliness, unhappiness and need to believe in something, had made him particularly susceptible to propaganda. It was at this time that he had started to listen to Russian broadcasts and read Russian literature, Mr Carman said, and so to espouse the cause of Soviet socialism.

For the next nine years, he continued, Geoff had clung to this cause, but during that time he'd been increasingly assailed by doubts about what he was doing, his first marriage had taken place and three years later failed, and he had been referred to a psychiatrist for severe depression.

The watershed, Mr Carman said, had been Geoff's marriage to me, which had been followed very quickly by his sudden resignation from GCHQ and then by two defection attempts which he hadn't been able to go through with because of me and the boys.

How vividly I still remembered one of those attempts. The other I had learned of later, from the police. I thought now as I'd thought many times before: *If he'd cared less about us, he might not be here today.*

I heard Mr Carman pointing out aspects of Geoff's behaviour which did not tally with his being a totally ruthless and rationally motivated spy.

First, he'd had the opportunity to defect and hadn't done so. Secondly, unlike Philby, Burgess and Maclean, he had not worked out with the Russians an escape route for himself. Also, he'd made no attempt to defect even after the police had seen him, when he could have done so and when he knew he was a suspect in sexual offences.

I thought back to the evening before Geoff's arrest when he'd left so abruptly and stayed out an hour. My husband had since told me that he'd gone away to think things through and, while doing so, had decided that, later in the evening, he would confess to me what he had done.

More painful, poignant memories were evoked for me as Mr Carman spoke of that confession and the agonising three weeks' struggle with my conscience resulting in my going to the authorities. This chain of events, he suggested, was unusual 'in a case of this extraordinary gravity'.

When first questioned by the police, Geoff had, he admitted, told lies, but this was because of wanting to serve a sentence that would 'enable him to keep a lifeline open with his wife and stepchildren, whom he loved and still does,' and then he had confessed to espionage and made a very full statement, thus providing all the evidence against himself.

'All that the Crown had,' he added, 'was the evidence of the mechanism by which he could transmit information and the mechanism by which he could receive it; what they had not got was the content of what was transmitted, when he had transmitted it, and to whom he had transmitted it.'

This aspect of the case, he felt, was very relevant to the question of sentence, as was the possible effect on other spies who might damage the country's security. If these people realised that their assistance in repairing that damage as soon as possible would be taken into account in any court charged with sentencing them, they would have an incentive to be cooperative. In being so cooperative Geoff had, Mr Carman said, hanged himself, since the damage assessment depended on the evaluation of his own account of what he had transmitted to the Soviet Intelligence Authority. He added that evidently these people did not think so highly of him as to have arranged any escape plan for him.

Mr Carman then queried the allegation that Geoff had persistently revealed important and secret matters over a period of fourteen years, since my husband, according to his statement, had had no contact with the Russian authorities from spring 1976 till spring 1980. Then, summoned by them to Vienna, he'd gone, taking with him material which he'd had since his resignation two and a half years earlier. Eighteen months later, they'd asked to see him again. This time he'd gone to Potsdam, where he'd been unable to give any further information and had simply answered questions put to him by a Russian Intelligence Officer. On both visits the Russians had done their best to persuade him to rejoin government service or even to try to join the Security Services but he had not complied with their suggestions.

Mr Carman therefore wished to submit that there were grounds for not passing 'the maximum kind of sentence for the worst sort of traitor'. Referring to Geoff, he continued, 'Your Lordship knows that he is forty-five next February, and I say humbly on his behalf: "How far into the twenty-first century has his sentence got to extend?"'

Then came the words which set my heart thumping madly: 'I now propose to call his wife who is anxious to give evidence on his behalf.' The Lord Chief Justice cut in to say that he would be willing to accept whatever Mr Carman might say on my behalf, should I not wish to give evidence.

'She wishes to give evidence,' Mr Carman replied and told the court that I had married Geoff in 1977 and, ever since he'd been taken into custody, had been regularly visiting my husband – who knew I had gone to the authorities about him but bore me no bitterness.

'This lady,' he continued, 'has received approaches from the national press with enormous sums of money, and takes the view as a practising Christian, as she is, that it would be immoral to make a profit out of her husband's treachery. She expressly asked me to say that after she has given evidence, she would be very grateful if the press would leave her and her family alone.'

Prompted by Sir Michael Havers, he concluded – to my surprise – 'The Attorney General reminds me that in today's *Daily Mail* there is a reference to Mrs Prime speaking to the newspaper last night in Gloucestershire. She has spoken to no newspaper. She has been in London, not in Cheltenham, did not speak to the newspaper and does not wish to do so.'

He stopped speaking, and I knew that the next move was up to me.

23

Witness

Knees knocking together, and very conscious of all the eminent, intelligent people watching me, I got up and walked to the witness box.

Passing self-consciously by the police, I wondered fleetingly whether my presence and the part I had played in bringing Geoff's espionage to light were sources of embarrassment to them. The next moment I entered the witness box – to the right of and on a level with the judge.

Turning away from the unnerving sea of faces below me, I looked across at Geoff – and we exchanged smiles, before a court official handed me a Bible and a small piece of paper. Nervously, haltingly, I read out the familiar words.

Duly sworn in, I looked at Mr Carman.

'I think you are a practising Christian, are you not?' he said.

'I am,' I replied.

He asked me how Geoff had treated me and the boys.

'With the utmost respect,' I said. For one panic-stricken moment, my mind went totally blank. Then, suddenly, the words and the confidence came. 'Geoff has been a good husband to me and a marvellous father figure for the boys,' I said, adding that he had worked hard and given us a standard of living much higher than the one we would otherwise have been able to enjoy.

Mr Carman spoke of the three weeks after Geoff's arrest. Had I taken advice on what to do and then informed the police of what I'd found and been told?

'Yes,' I replied. 'Morally, I felt it was something I had to do. As a Christian I couldn't have that on my conscience or my husband's conscience, either. I believe in the end I will have done him a favour and hopefully the country a favour too.'

How did Geoff react when he learnt that I had gone to the authorities, Mr Carman asked.

'He has taken it very well,' I said, and went on to speak of how my husband had changed since losing the dreadful burden he had been carrying for so long.

'Up till now he's been a tortured personality. Now he's learning to relate to people.'

'Do you intend to stand by him, Mrs Prime?'

'Yes. As a Christian I can only utterly condemn the terrible crimes he has committed, but equally as a Christian I can forgive him because he's repentant and remorseful, I believe.'

The Attorney General had no questions for me. I walked back to my place and sat down, feeling spent but at peace. My words had not had the eloquence of Mr Carman or Sir Michael Havers, but they had come straight from my heart and included my Christian faith and belief. I was certain that God had been with me – and that he still was.

It was time for the Lord Chief Justice to pass sentence, and we all stood to hear what he had to say.

He had listened, he said, to all that Mr Carman had said on Geoff's behalf, but the court had also heard enough to realise that his treachery had done 'incalculable harm to the interests of security of this country and the interests of security of our friends and allies'.

His words sounded ominous. I listened in growing apprehension as he continued, 'What exactly motivated you no one will ever know for certain, but it may have been what was doubtless called "ideological reasons", and I am asked by Mr Carman not to treat you or to consider you as a ruthless or rationally motivated spy.'

Aghast, I heard him sum up his own reactions in one damning sentence: 'I am bound to say that that is a description that fits you exactly.'

He gave credit to Geoff for confessing to the police, for pleading guilty and for furnishing the prosecution with most of their material, he said. Hope flickered again, only to be extinguished by his next words: 'You must suffer the results of the choice you made. The result is designed to punish you; it is designed to mark the public abhorrence for the crimes you have committed, and finally, of course, to deter others who may "toy" with the idea of treachery in the future.'

I could barely contain the turmoil inside me as he proceeded to pass sentence. On each count or group of counts he apportioned numbers of years to be served. The figures sounded alarmingly high and seemed to be coming thick and fast.

Then came the unforgettable, devastating words: 'The total therefore will be thirty-eight years. Let him go down.'

I collapsed in a heap and started to cry.

Almost at once a policewoman helped me out of the courtroom and she and others pushed a way for me through the ranks of waiting pressmen, and brought me back into the room where I'd spent the adjournment.

There I broke into hysterical weeping. Dimly I was aware that there were people around me, trying to help and comfort.

'Was it much worse than you'd expected?' one of them asked, solicitously.

'Oh, yes,' I sobbed vehemently, thinking, *What a question!*

Jane arrived, having been escorted from the gallery by a burly policeman, and sat beside me – putting her arm round my shoulders. Mr Hirst and Mr Bowden followed. It was a relief to be with friends rather than strangers and their concern and care were obvious, but I couldn't stop crying and the anguish inside me wasn't easing at all.

A strong cup of tea was put into my shaking hands. I managed to gulp it down.

After a while Mr Bowden said, 'We are not at your husband's funeral. He is alive and downstairs and you will soon be able to see him.'

That thought, more than any other, helped me to battle for some degree of self-control and calmness.

Mr Carman came in looking sad and concerned.

'I think we tackled it in the only possible way,' he told me. 'If anything could have helped, what you said would have done. I think we should appeal – we certainly have nothing to lose. Think about it and let me know. We have to decide within twenty-eight days. I'll go and see your husband now, and when you feel ready to, you can go and see him too.'

'What can we do about the press and all their false stories?' I asked.

'I'm afraid you cannot sue for libel on legal aid,' he told me.

So the newspapers would virtually be able to print what they liked, I thought. When Mr Carman had gone, I tried to prepare myself for going to see Geoff. What state would he be in, I wondered. And how would I cope?

After a while I felt ready to try. I was taken downstairs and into the deeper recesses of the building. Behind large locked doors, which were opened to admit me, was a big brick-walled room. I was shown to one of the bench seats in it and on sitting there, found myself looking at Geoff through a window. It was torment not being able to touch him on that day above all.

We looked at one another. Geoff seemed amazingly composed.

'You were wonderful,' he said.

'Thank you,' I replied. 'God helped me. I could never have done what I did without him.'

Geoff said, 'I'm sorry – but I forgot to read that psalm you wanted me to.' I felt disappointed, but tried not to show it. He asked me what I thought about an appeal.

Feeling in no fit state to make decisions about such important matters, I said, 'I'm not sure. I'll have to think and pray about that. I'm going away for a while because of the press, but I'll come and see you soon. Have you any idea where you'll be?'

'Long Lartin,' he said.

My face lit up instantly. Long Lartin is in the Vale of Evesham, only about fifteen miles from Cheltenham. It had seemed too much to hope that he'd be sent there straight away.

I later learnt that no prisoner had ever been sent direct to Long Lartin after his trial. Geoff had expected to go initially to a London prison.

'That's fantastic,' I said. 'An answer to prayer, I believe.'

'I like your hat,' Geoff said, adding humorously, 'Very Cheltenham.' I laughed, still marvelling at his calmness. His next words gave me a clue to his real feelings.

'Mind you, in my state of mind today, I'd probably like anything.'

We were allowed about half an hour together. Parting, with a decision hanging over us and not knowing when we'd meet again, was more painful than ever.

Jane, Mr Hirst and Mr Bowden were waiting for me in a downstairs corridor near a back entrance.

'There are about four hundred representatives of the press outside, but we've worked out a plan to avoid them,' they said.

Some friendly officials escorted us to the back door.

'Last people out of here were Thorpe and the Ripper's wife,' remarked one of them as she let us out. Hurriedly, we crossed the pavement, shielded by a double wall of tall policemen standing shoulder to shoulder, and climbed into a waiting taxi which drove off immediately, taking us round to the front of the building first of all.

Through the window I could see the press, a seething mass of them, standing by the main entrance or on the steps leading up to it. I felt unnerved to realise that they were waiting for me and at the same time pleased and relieved that we had foiled them.

Or most of them. Even as I watched, some, realising what had happened, came rushing towards the taxi, cameras poised. I ducked, willing the traffic lights showing red just ahead to change quickly, which they did.

We zoomed off and out of reach of even the most fleet-footed and dedicated newsmen.

Mr Bowden and Mr Hirst started talking together and so did Jane and I. She told me that as she'd seen and heard me in the witness box, she'd been overwhelmingly convinced that God had been specially with me. I had been very aware of this too.

Not surprisingly, the media came up for discussion, and in the course of conversation Jane said, 'In the tube we saw a picture of you with the headline, "Spy's wife stands by her husband," but Mr Bowden told us not to mention it to you till after the trial.'

I sighed heavily at the thought of having to cope with all the additional strains that the press would no doubt cause us in the coming weeks.

The taxi dropped us back at the flat where we stayed for a little while. I spent the time recovering, phoning home and getting ready for the journey to Cheltenham.

Mr Bowden drove. It was good to have Jane and the others to talk or listen to on the long drive. My feelings were strangely mixed. At one level, I felt devastated and grief stricken. At another, I was aware of the extraordinary peace I had known, in some measure, all along.

Mr Carman had said everything possible – fluently and persuasively. Many people had been praying earnestly. And yet the sentence had surpassed my worst nightmares. It seemed utterly disproportionate to give three years for the sexual offences as compared with *thirty-five* for the spying – and this certainly didn't reflect the relative degrees of anguish experienced. But that was how the judge had allocated sentence, totalling a staggering thirty-eight years. Why? God alone knew but I still trusted him, though feebly and painfully.

Somewhere along the route we overtook a police van and I thought, *What if Geoff's in there – being taken to Long Lartin!* It gave me the strangest, saddest feeling to pass the van and then leave it far behind.

To avoid the press I stayed in Jane's home in Cheltenham

until dark, telephoning my parents and Peter from there to find out about the boys. I had arranged to stay with my parents so, when we judged it safe, Jane's husband drove me round, calling at Peter's on the way to see Mark and Stephen. They seemed to be coping remarkably well.

We arrived at mum and dad's safely. Craig took one look at me and burst into tears. I put him to bed and talked and prayed with him until he seemed calmer. My parents were very shaken up, having seen the trial on television and then had the press to contend with. Reporters and cameramen had hung around for hours, trying to get into or inveigle someone out of the house, in the hope of obtaining a story. One of them had even asked to use the toilet in my parents' house. Fortunately, my father isn't that gullible.

We went to bed eventually and I fell into an exhausted sleep.

At half past twelve the phone rang. My father dragged himself out of bed and went to answer it. There was a reporter at the other end wanting to know if it was true that Geoffrey Prime had had a heart attack and would be spending the rest of his prison sentence in hospital.

Dad replied that he had heard no such news and rang off, feeling shocked and worried. He came and told mum and myself what had happened. I felt sure that this was a ploy to get some reaction from us and was really shattered at the thought that another human being, knowing what we had been through that day, could stoop to such tactics. We went back to bed to try and get some sleep.

In the morning we learnt that Mr Davies had also been roused from sleep by a caller asking the same question.

It was on this day, as I discovered later, that the Prime Minister made a statement in the House of Commons to the effect that she had decided to refer my husband's case to the Security Commission, asking it to investigate possible breaches in security and advise, if necessary, on changes in security arrangements. The Security Commission started work towards the end of November and continued its investigations until the following May.

Soon after the trial, in order to avoid the newsmen and recover a little, our family went to ground for about a week – Stephen and Mark staying with friends and Craig and I with our Cheshire relatives. Once again our host and hostess could not have been kinder, though we must have been poor company.

I felt I had to face the press accounts of the trial and the relevant articles, and braced myself to read them. There was an enormous amount to read, as we seemed to be front page news in all the papers for some time. As I tried to take in some of what had been written, I found myself gripped at times by a feeling of unreality. The picture that emerged of the world powers expending colossal resources on watching one another, was one that I found very disturbing.

Bemusedly I read of NASA and GCHQ projects involving the setting up of satellites which could photograph Soviet military installations, record the results of their missile tests and penetrate their military computer system; eavesdrop on any part of the microwave network on which their telephone system was based and intercept short-wave radio conversations. Evidently, through what Geoff and two American spies, Boyce and Lee, had reported or handed over to their Soviet contacts, the KGB had been made aware of these aspects of the western surveillance system.

I read of these things with a very heavy heart. In the end, a totally one-sided picture was presented of both Geoff and me. Underneath a close-up photograph showing my face with a misleading smile on it, I read an account of what I had worn, said and done at the trial. It was accurate enough, but none of the inner agony came through at all. The true human story could never be told in that way, I thought.

It was daunting to realise that the reports and articles I was reading and many others – some, no doubt, inaccurate even in matters of fact – were being read throughout the country. And the newspapers of other countries round the world would be covering the 'story' in a variety of ways too.

One thing that did please me was that every British

newspaper which I saw made some mention of what I had said about my Christian faith.

On Sunday evening I was due to visit Geoff at Long Lartin for the first time. Our relations drove Craig and me to the Vale of Evesham where my parents met us. There we said our goodbyes and drove our separate ways – back to Cheshire or on to the prison.

24

Dual sentence

We had trouble finding Long Lartin in the growing darkness. Then we noticed an orange glow in the sky and drove towards it. Sure enough there lay the vast prison complex with the enormous lights above it. These and the massive dome-topped walls made it look to me like something from outer space. Also visible was the silhouetted tip of a church spire.

We drove into the car park. Once mum, dad and Craig had seen me enter the check-in area, they went in search of a local church service.

It was quickly obvious to me that the security system and procedures at Long Lartin were different from any I'd come across before. Here everything was computerised and electronic, with closed circuit television and shortwave radio, and all the necessary screens, gadgets and buttons.

I was taken through several enormous heavy doors and across an open grassy area to the inner prison. The opening of one door, I noticed, would automatically seal off the others in the vicinity. Some were opened by keys but most were operated by remote control from the central office, in response to the voice of the official requesting clearance by speaking into a little box on the wall.

Geoff, I knew, was in the hospital wing, isolated from most of the other prisoners. I climbed some stairs and was admitted past more doors and escorted along more corridors.

What state would my husband be in, I wondered. After the trial he had been amazing but perhaps the enormity of the sentence hadn't sunk in by then.

As I approached his room, I heard singing. Evidently a service was in progress in the church whose spire I had seen above the prison walls. It was a beautiful sound to hear just then, reminding me of God's presence even in this place.

Geoff's face lit up when he saw me and we hugged one another. Through his window I could see a floodlit football pitch and some trees. I was glad that he had such a view.

A guard brought in an easy chair for me and went out again. I sat down. Apart from the wooden chair on which Geoff was seated, there were a hospital-type bed and a desk piled high with books and writing materials. As usual there were no electrical points but the window looked unusual, the bars being sandwiched between two solid-looking panes. Perhaps this was what was called a suicide cell.

I shuddered inwardly at the thought that Geoff had been put here because the authorities feared that he might take his own life. Would he do such a thing, I wondered, in acute alarm. In these circumstances I couldn't be sure of the answer.

'Once again, there's nothing to do all day except read, write and think,' my husband said.

The trial was still uppermost in our minds and we shared our shock and devastation and tried to comfort each other.

A guard brought in tea. We drank it and ate a little of the food which I had brought from Cheshire.

We had to try to think about an appeal. Should we or shouldn't we ask for one? It seemed very soon to have to decide about this. We talked it over for a while and then I left it to Geoff to make the final decision.

We must have had about an hour and a half together before I said goodbye. In the circumstances, it was a surprisingly good visit.

That evening Mark, Stephen, Craig and I were together again in Laburnham Cottage. As a family and as individuals we would have to try and pick up the threads of our lives.

About ten days later a probation officer rang to tell me that Geoff had decided to go ahead with the appeal. Mr Davies had been among those who had felt that we should proceed with it; at any rate, he and others added, we had nothing to lose. And so that decision was made. I had mixed feelings about it but my busy life gave me little time for brooding about that or anything else. That was a good thing, as was the fact that I had to force myself to think about and tackle all sorts of jobs. But I was often almost overcome by exhaustion as I tried to be a mother and housewife, as well as a wife to someone whom I could only see for a couple of hours once a fortnight and must otherwise communicate with through letters – which were vetted and which had never been my forte anyway. Somehow, through these means, we managed to build on our relationship.

Geoff was kept for four and a half months in the hospital wing although he was not ill; nor, so he assured me later, did he ever think of suicide. But the prison authorities presumably felt they could not take the risk of putting him elsewhere. He only had superficial contact with other prisoners in the hospital and was under constant escort.

In contrast, I was seeing many people. A whole host of them had come into my life in the past months, some in an official capacity, others as friends. Visits, letters or phone calls to or from these people took up much time but it was well worth it. Many of the officials whom I met were sympathetic, helpful and generous with their time, and the love, support and prayers of my newer friends, along with those of the 'old faithfuls', kept me going.

On top of all this were the letters from strangers. After the trial, they poured in from all over the country. Almost every county was represented. A tiny percentage of writers were critical of me. One even said that I deserved the noose around my neck for betraying my husband. But by far the majority were kind and supportive.

Non-Christians wrote, unable to understand how I could possibly stand by Geoff but deeply moved by it none the less. Christians wrote to say they felt I was showing true Christianity – Christianity in action – and promised prayer.

Some people expressed their deep understanding of Geoff's sexual problems, through having similar problems themselves. They could not condone what he had done, but they could identify with him.

One treasured letter was from the mother of a girl whom Geoff had telephoned. She was a Christian, she said, and completely forgave Geoff for what he had done. In fact, she and her friends were praying for us.

In another letter, a man quoted, 'Let him who is without sin cast the first stone,' and 'There, but for the grace of God, go I.'

Many sent money or offered all kinds of gifts, including holidays.

The boys and I were touched and encouraged by this massive vote of confidence as well as by people's generosity and their promises of prayer and support. Little by little, as I could afford the stamps, the stationery and the time, I wrote replies, thanking people for their kindness.

Geoff received a few letters, too. Some were from people he had known in the past, others from strangers. Since then they have continued to keep in touch – ready to help in any way they can.

An organisation about which I knew very little sent me a warm, kind letter. It was called the Prison Christian Fellowship and had a large membership of Christians inside and outside prisons. I decided to join the local branch and started going to meetings and receiving the national newsletter. It was thrilling to meet and hear about people dedicated to showing God's love to people in prison and to learn about so-called hardened criminals being completely changed through committing their lives to Jesus Christ.

People's reactions in person were very similar to the written ones – in that the vast majority were kind and tactful and a small minority hostile or insensitive. There were those who stopped outside our house to stare and point out 'the spy's house', or those who painted 'USSR', 'the Soviet Union' and similar slogans, in white spray paint, along the wall down our lane.

There was also the press to cope with. Once again they swarmed all over Cheltenham, hoping for a story. As before, they hung round outside our house and bothered my parents and friends. Unwisely, breaking my usual rule, I spoke to one of them about the letters I'd received, emphasising how few had been condemning and how many supportive. I thought this would make a harmless, heartwarming story.

Not a bit of it. The next day, reading what the reporter had written, I was horrified to find that he had slanted his report to make it sound as though the reaction had been negative. Evidently the press, as usual, had deemed that bad news made for a better story than good news.

Other stories were published about Geoff and myself. Almost all contained inaccuracies – some minor, others highly damaging. We had no way of refuting them effectively.

According to one story, my husband had been blackmailing colleagues at GCHQ. An irate Geoff assured me that he had always worked alone and would not have contemplated blackmail even if it had been possible. I believed him, even before a letter came confirming this. Later, the Report of the Security Commission of May 1983 stated: '. . . we have received no evidence to substantiate the allegation widely reported in the press on 17 January 1983 that Prime was blackmailing some of his colleagues.' Mr Davies and I then tackled the papers concerned. Some of them printed a small apology in their next editions.

Then came the *News of the World* story. It said that my husband, using an alias, had made espionage contacts through a child-sex network in Britain and America.

Geoff was totally incensed by this article.

'This is too much! We can't let them get away with it,' he said. He had never joined or had anything to do with either of the organisations named in the paper, he told me – and I believed him and felt sickened and angry about what had happened.

All we could do was contact Mr Davies and ask him to write to the Press Council denying the allegation and making a complaint about the story. Geoff's solicitor undertook to do this and wrote the first of several letters to this body.

Not quite all the representatives of the press or media whom we encountered caused us extra heartache, anger or frustration. I remember chatting to a very kind lady journalist about my life since the trial, and she sent me a beautiful bouquet, which arrived at a time when I was feeling particularly low. This touched me, as did the sympathetic letter I received from the television reporter who'd been courteous enough to leave us alone before the trial when asked to do so.

Meanwhile life in Long Lartin and Laburnham Cottage went on. My visits to Geoff were by no means all as positive and calm as the first one had been. We both went through black times. Whenever this happened to me, sooner or later some form of help or encouragement would come my way.

Once at such a time I received a letter from Geoff. Referring to the day of his arrest, he wrote, 'I have an indelible picture of you in my mind – waving and smiling as I was driven away on that fateful day. Even then you were wonderful.'

Wonderful! I thought, staring at the word in amazement. I had felt terrible, desperate – anything but wonderful. But it cheered me up to know that my husband had seen in me that way, both for his own sake and because it confirmed to me the fact that I had been given, although not realising it at the time, a strength beyond my own.

One of Geoff's low patches occurred early in the New Year.

25

Holding on

On a visiting day in January, two guards came and sat in the room with us, instead of sitting outside as previously. We found this very inhibiting. While they had been outside, albeit with the door ajar and within sight and sound of us, we had coped reasonably well, appreciating the necessity of such supervision. But having them actually in the room was a different matter.

As time went on and the practice continued we – Geoff particularly – found the situation almost intolerable. Above all he deeply resented any implication that I could not be trusted, he said.

One day he told me, 'I can't cope with this. I've got to make a stand about it. Perhaps you shouldn't come and visit me for a while. In this situation we'll never be able to discuss anything personal.'

My heart sank. Visits and letters were the lifeblood of our relationship. If we were to stop seeing one another or if Geoff were to refuse to discuss anything personal so long as the guards were present in the room, there'd very soon *be* no relationship between us.

I told a small prayer group at the church about the problem and we started to pray together for God to act.

Quite soon I received a letter from Geoff saying he *did* want me to come on the next visit. I felt cheered. Even if we only talked about business and practical matters, this would be better than not meeting at all.

At the prison, after the preliminaries, I was escorted along the familiar hospital corridor towards Geoff's room. Looking up, I saw him, smiling as he came to meet me. Amazed and delighted, I hurried to greet him.

He led me to his room and we went in and sat down.

'The guards are going to sit outside today. Psychologically that makes all the difference,' he said. I agreed, beaming.

'Right up to lunch time they said they were going to be in the room with us,' he continued, 'and I was getting into a state because I wanted to see you and talk, but after what I'd said last time, I didn't feel I would be able to. Then, half an hour ago, while I was trying to eat my dinner, they came in and said there'd been a change. They didn't give a reason, so I don't know what's going on at all!'

'I do,' I said brightly. 'We prayed about it.' Geoff's face told me that this version of events didn't make sense to him but he was just as overjoyed as I was that we could talk with a greater sense of privacy and freedom.

It was a good meeting. Afterwards he said, 'This will be a "one-off". We won't be able to do this again, but please come next time anyway.'

'All right,' I said aloud while thinking, *Right, Lord, I'm going to have another prayer about this*.

Over the next fortnight I told my friends what had happened. Just as I had done and as people so often do when God answers their prayers, they felt a mixture of amazement, elation and awe. All of them were keen to pray that the guards would not be in the room with us at the next meeting, so that Geoff and I could continue to sort out more personal matters.

The day of my next visit came. Feeling torn between doubt and faith, I went through the usual checking and waiting procedures before being escorted to Geoff's room.

I found my husband alone.

'The guards aren't going to be here again,' he said, sounding pleased but mystified. I could hardly contain my delight and we had another worthwhile meeting.

When I reported back to my friends they were ecstatic. One said, 'Once might have been a coincidence but twice —

no way! That *has* to be God's doing.' We all agreed
wholeheartedly and were encouraged to keep praying for
God to act in all our lives.

The more I thought about this incident, the more I
marvelled. It wasn't as though Geoff were serving a short-
term sentence in a local prison. He was a category A prisoner,
serving an extremely long sentence in a maximum security
prison, and up till then the security surrounding him had
been phenomenal. Even the police had commented on it –
one of them saying to me, 'I've never seen anything like it in
my life.'

I felt humble, grateful and encouraged. If God could do
what he had just done, he could do anything, no matter how
impossible the situation might look from the human view-
point.

On my next visit to Geoff, the guards were back in the
room with us, saying it had all been a mistake, but by then,
our relationship having been put on to a better footing, Geoff
and I were more able to cope with the situation.

For some time I had been considering whether to write a
book based on the journal I had been keeping – begun soon
after Geoff's arrest. Mr Bowden, Mr Glass and others had
been encouraging me to think and pray about this possibility.
If I did write a story, it would have to contain the truth as I
saw it and be done in conjunction with people whom I could
trust.

I prayed that if God wanted such a book to be written, he
would guide me through a chain of events. I was put in touch
with Pastor John Lancaster, editor of the magazine for the
Elim churches, called the Elim Evangel. He knew Edward
England, a Christian literary agent. The agent, feeling very
dubious about the project, came to see and talk with me. He
suggested that we should both pray over the matter for some
time.

A few days later, much sooner than I'd anticipated, I
received a letter from him. He supported my decision not to
sell my story to a newspaper, however high the fee, but

believed that over the next year I should quietly go ahead with the writing of this book. God was giving me a little nudge and soon I was being introduced to an editor at Hodder & Stoughton. To this meeting the agent brought Jean Watson, a writer, who might work alongside me. After a second meeting with her, I knew that God had been leading me step by step to the right agent and publisher, and to a writer who would become my good friend.

After that, the writing of the book was to take up much of my time, thought and energy, and to cause deep pain and healing.

At the end of March, Geoff was taken out of the hospital wing and transferred to normal accommodation. He was allocated a job in one of the prison workshops and worked, like everyone else, mornings and afternoons, starting at eight o'clock. From five to six o'clock, after the evening meal, prisoners would be locked by electronic means into their cells but after that, from six to nine o'clock, they would be able to move about within a small area of the prison and watch television, play board games, attend a service or whatever. Then from nine until seven the following morning they'd be back in their cells – locked up again.

Life in the main wings was much noisier, with televisions blaring out their programmes and radios their pop music. But at least the guards sat outside the small room in which I now visited Geoff.

'You seem to be going to a lot of meetings and doing a good deal of praying these days,' my husband remarked to me one day after I'd been telling him about what I'd been doing.

'Yes,' I said. 'I've become a committed Christian.' With a puzzled look, he remarked, 'But you always were a Christian.' By that he meant, I expect, that I was a church-goer and a law-abiding citizen!

'I used to go to church sometimes,' I agreed. 'But Christianity didn't mean much to me. Now it's my whole life.'

He gave me a thoughtful look and didn't pursue the matter.

Craig often used to ask to visit and finally I agreed. It was moving to see how pleased he and Geoff were to see one another, and the two talked like old friends.

Afterwards Craig told me happily, 'That's my first prayer answered.'

Later, when he was accepted to go to the Grammar School where his brothers were, he was to say, 'That's my second prayer answered.'

An answer to one of my prayers was the passing of my driving test. Strangely enough the ten pounds which I'd handed in to the police in May, and received back after the trial in November, helped to pay for this. At last I was able to drive the Mini. Inevitably, I soon found myself driving round too much and trying to fit in too many things.

Geoff seemed to be coping well, considering his situation and the sentence. His interviews with the Security Services, which had begun in late November, were still going on and didn't in fact end until May.

Meanwhile the appeal started to loom large in my thoughts and friends prayed with me about this event due to take place on April 21st. I dreaded the thought of all the exposure and publicity again, but began to hope for great things. As I kept telling Geoff, we had told the truth so at the appeal we would surely be given tangible credit for that. Of one thing I was absolutely certain. If God wanted my husband's sentence to be cut, he would find a way of doing it.

Feeling desperately in need of a break, I arranged for Craig to stay with an aunt and Stephen with friends, and left Mark in charge of the house for one night while I went away on my own.

On my return I was in for a terrible shock. The boys had had a party for their friends and some gatecrashers had pushed their way in. The resultant chaos and damage was horrifying. A carpet was burnt, a window broken, and there were other evidences that the event had got horribly out of hand.

It was the proverbial last straw, and the panic I felt, along with many pent-up emotions, was expressed in an outburst of anger which alarmed not only the boys, already upset at what had happened, but also me – so much so that I nearly drove myself to the local psychiatric hospital to get some help. Instead of doing that, however, I made a desperate effort to calm down and carry on as best I could.

A few days later Craig arrived home in an unhappy state. He said he didn't like coming back to our house because it gave him a horrible feeling. His words reminded me of what someone else had said. This man, one of the few press or media people who had shown real concern for us, had been in our home not long before this and had commented on the oppressive atmosphere. Himself a Christian, he had prayed with me about the matter.

Now, suddenly, he rang up to ask whether I'd checked on the boys' records. I had, but not very thoroughly. After his phone call I went and investigated properly.

What I found shook me. Some of the records had definite occult overtones. Their covers had horrific or even blasphemous lyrics or both.

I rang Mr Glass, and he promised to come round the following day and speak to the boys.

After a bad night I woke early in a state of utter turmoil about the whole situation and felt that I had to get out by myself. I dressed quickly, then left the house, got into my car and drove myself to Cleeve Hill, parking in the place where the whole devastating chain of events had begun just over a year earlier. Once again I was overwhelmed by churning emotions in the midst of lovely, quiet surroundings. But this time I cried out to God and read my Bible.

Gradually, the storm inside me died down. The aching grief that I now lived with was still there, but back came the peace and assurance of God's presence and love.

Mr Glass's arrival later in the day proved an added strength. He explained to Mark and Stephen why occult records were undesirable and illustrated the point with true stories. I told the boys that I didn't want such records in the house and said that I believed they were affecting the atmosphere, if nothing else.

Reluctantly my two older sons removed the questionable records, giving them to friends or selling them – neither of which were ideal solutions, but I felt too frayed to insist on stronger measures. My parents and a couple of friends generously gave the boys money to buy new and more acceptable records to replace some of the ones they'd had to dispose of.

Mark, Stephen and their friends agreed among themselves and afterwards told me, quite amiably, that in their opinion I had 'flipped my lid' about this matter. However, later I became even more convinced of the dangers of this type of music.

Meanwhile, with the appeal less than a week away, I felt very relieved at the clean sweep we had made and prayed frequently, alone and with my mother and friends, for the coming crucial event.

26

Appeal

The Royal Courts of Justice, from the outside, resembled a cathedral, I thought, and looked quite striking on the morning of April 21st, with the sun shining on its white stone walls and spires.

Once inside the building we were shown into the courtroom where Geoff's 'application for leave to appeal against sentence', as it was officially called, was to be heard. My husband was not to be present at the proceedings. We had been advised that his being there would ensure maximum publicity – which would not help the case at all. So, reluctantly, Geoff had agreed not to go and had asked me to be there instead. So here I was, feeling very weak, vulnerable and apprehensive.

Sunlight filtered through the arched windows of the room where I was sitting. On one side of me was the friend who had said she would be with me – Jean Watson; on the other was Mr Davies. Beside and behind us were men and women representing the press, the police and the Security Services. In front and below were Mr Carman and Mr Clover appearing for the applicant, Geoff, and Mr Richardson and Mr Coward appearing for the Crown. I had spoken to our defence counsel for a few moments in the corridor before coming into the courtroom and they had been as friendly and helpful as ever. But now they and the other two barristers seemed remote and set apart from the rest of us – perhaps mainly because of their distinctive legal uniform.

The scene brought the trial vividly to mind and I found myself battling with similar doubts and fears.

Would I be able to cope with the ordeal ahead? What would the outcome be? I thought of all those who would be deeply affected by today's decision: Geoff in Long Lartin, the boys, the rest of my family, and my friends. Would today bring the realisation or crushing of all our hopes and prayers?

At half-past ten a hush fell on the court and my apprehension became even more acute. We rose to our feet and the judges entered and took their places on the raised platform in front of us. Lord Justice Lawton seated himself in the central chair, with his colleagues – Mr Justice Michael Davies and Sir Roger Ormrod – on either side. Under their wigs, their bespectacled faces looked expressionless.

When everyone was seated Mr Carman rose and began to speak on Geoff's behalf. As I listened I kept praying to God to be present and in control. Jean, I knew, was doing the same, while Mr Davies took copious notes.

Mr Carman stressed first the extreme length of the sentence – the longest passed on anyone of any age for the past twenty years and the longest on anyone aged forty-four for very many more years than that. Then, having expressed his respect for the Lord Chief Justice and added that he did not question the seriousness of the case, he asked whether there were other legitimate aims of sentencing policy which had not been taken into consideration at the trial.

In Geoff's case he felt that it was relevant to consider how the offences had been uncovered and the attitude of 'the applicant' since then. In this connection he drew the court's attention to eleven factors. One of these was that my husband had resigned from GCHQ in 1977, four and a half years before the offences had come to light, and had made no attempt to rejoin government service thereafter.

The tragedy of it all struck me again as I listened. Geoff had told me that disclosure had come at a time when he felt he had finished with his double life – so much so that he had grown careless and had therefore left some of the tools of his trade lying around. But, I thought, it was at this juncture that my husband's sexual problems had come to a head . . .

Mr Carman was now pointing out that Geoff had confessed his sexual problems as well as his spying, first to me and then to the police. The detailed statement he had made concerning his espionage must have been enormously valuable to the Security Services, Mr Carman said, adding that it was this which had made possible the drawing up of the seven counts on the first indictment.

'If not for that detail, how many counts would there have been?' he asked, and gave the answer: 'There may have been one rather than seven.'

Yes, I thought, *and if there had been one count, he would have been given up to a maximum of fourteen years, instead of thirty-five!* Geoff and I had spoken about this – he particularly mentioning the count in connection with his November trip. For this he had been given seven years, although – he assured me – he had passed on nothing new.

Mr Carman was informing the court that since the previous November my husband had made himself fully available for thirteen interviews with the Security Services, lasting some thirty-seven hours.

His words were persuasive and yet I sensed that all was not well – a feeling accentuated when, in response to Mr Carman's point that Geoff had worked alone and had therefore not caused the deaths of others, Lord Justice Lawton interposed cryptically, 'In the past.'

'As you say, in the past,' agreed Mr Carman, who then suggested that far more credit should be given to spies who cooperate with the authorities, where the only information known to the police is the raw material which comes from them.

He would like the court, he said, not to forget to give incentives to future traitors and their relatives to be cooperative, adding some words which pained me deeply: 'A sentence which stretches until a person is eighty-two provides no incentive to cooperate or confess.'

A moment later, Lord Justice Lawton announced that the

proceedings would continue *in camera* and named the few people who were to be permitted to attend that.

My friend and I left the courtroom with Mr Davies, only to be confronted by the press. Jean and I escaped down some stairs and into a ladies' toilet.

Standing by the washbasins, with our backs to the people coming in and out, we shared our fears about the way things seemed to be going.

'Give me something,' I urged, thrusting my New Testament into Jean's hands. She found and we read together some verses about God being able to bring good out of any situation for those who loved him.

'Lord, help us to believe this. Keep your promise,' we whispered.

A woman member of the press whom I had met and liked, came across to shake my hand and wish me all the best, and then went quickly out.

We went back upstairs. An official saw us and told us we could wait in the courtroom since the *in camera* session was being held in an inner chamber. Mr Davies, Jean and I went back in and sat down. We talked but it was merely to fill in time. After about an hour others came in again, including Mr Carman and Mr Clover. They looked up at me with unsmiling expressions which confirmed my sense of foreboding. I leant across the intervening seats towards them and Mr Carman said, 'Rhona, I'm afraid you'll have to prepare yourself for the worst. They were polite, but that was all.'

I sank back into my place, feeling crushed.

'No hope?' Jean asked quietly. I shook my head and fought for self-control.

The judges returned and took their places and then Mr Carman stood up and pressed bravely on. He alluded to the fact that some spies were given immunity and some stripped of their honours. My husband, he said, had not been given immunity and had not defected when he'd had the opportunity to do so. He proceeded to emphasise some of his earlier arguments, but I feared that the writing was on the wall. Feeling suddenly faint, I sipped some water.

At lunch time Lord Justice Lawton called for a one-and-a-half hour adjournment – to allow for a thorough discussion, he said.

Was this a hopeful sign, I wondered. But how was I going to get through every suspense filled minute of that time?

The three of us left the courtroom and were joined by Mr Carman and Mr Clover. The newsmen and women were obviously going to follow us, whichever way we turned. Mr Carman tried confrontation.

'Look,' he said, facing them squarely and speaking in firm tones, 'Mrs Prime is not available for interviews and you know very well that photographs may not be taken within the premises, so will you please leave her alone?'

With that we walked away, hoping to find within the buildings a place where refreshments could be obtained. The press followed. We twisted and turned quite a bit but they were always a few paces behind.

At last we found what we were looking for – but a notice told us that the place was closed pending alterations.

We moved off again, as did our rearguard.

'They're not going to give up,' Mr Carman said. He and Mr Clover consulted briefly, then took us down to the barristers' robing room. A few barristers shot astonished looks at Jean and me as if to say, *Women – in here!?* But at least we were safe from the press. The question was – how were we to get out and have some lunch? Not that I was hungry.

An official was consulted. He thought he could get us out through a back door, and led us to it. We looked out. There was not a camera in sight so, leaving Mr Carman and Mr Clover behind, the three of us slipped into the street and walked quickly away to the nearest snack bar.

I went downstairs to find and keep a table while the other two queued for food at the counter. They came down a little later with plates of quiche and salad. As we ate, or tried to, we talked surreptitiously about the proceedings – afraid of eavesdroppers.

We tried to be cheerful but couldn't hide from each other the fact that none of us hoped for anything dramatic to happen. But any reduction of the sentence would be something, I thought, and kept hoping at least for that.

Walking back afterwards, we suddenly found ourselves the centre of press attention again. Cameramen rushed towards us.

'I'm sorry,' said one of them, snapping away.

'No you're not,' Jean retorted. 'Or you wouldn't be doing this.' I tried to hide my face as we walked along as quickly as possible. Our entourage kept pace with us, pressing me to pose or throwing out the 'How-are-you?' type of question.

One said, 'Would you please stand for me, Mrs Prime?'

'No, I won't stand for you,' I said crossly. 'And I never have stood for any of you.'

At last we were near enough to make a dash for the door – heads down.

A moment later we were in the courtroom again. I sat on a bench feeling breathless and in dread of the coming session.

The court duly reassembled and Lord Justice Lawton, in slow, emphatic tones, began to deliver his judgment.

First he outlined the offences and the sentence given for them, and then reviewed the sequence of events leading up to Geoff's arrest and on to his confession and statement to the police.

A brief résumé of my husband's working life and espionage activities followed. Then came the ominous statement that he agreed with the Lord Chief Justice's assessment of the damage he had caused.

His next words sounded more promising and hope flared briefly in me as he stated his willingness to accept that as a result of my husband's cooperation some of the damage might be able to be repaired, and added that he had also weighed what had been said about incentive to future spies and their families.

The thirteen interviews with the Security Services, however, he said, were a matter to be taken into account on the parole review rather than by the court.

'The court,' he continued, 'has to consider the objectives of sentencing the offender before the court. These can be put as retribution, deterrence, rehabilitation and prevention.'

All hope died as I heard him add, 'In this case we can ignore the last two.'

He told us that in modern sentencing policy the court had to reflect the abhorrence that right-minded members of the public felt. The Lord Chief Justice had been right, he said, to speak of 'public abhorrence'. Geoff had taken the Queen's shilling and betrayed her and her allies to their enemies. In wartime his crime would have merited the death penalty, he pointed out. As it was, justice had to be meted out not only to the 'Admiral Byngs' but also to those lower down the government scale.

Then came his final words. The Lord Chief Justice's sentence at the trial should stand. The application for leave to appeal was dismissed.

27

In the depths

Shock and anger carried me through the next few hours but underneath was sheer anguish.

I walked in a daze through the corridors, flanked by Jean, Mr Davies and our two barristers.

'No photographs, no interviews,' Mr Carman told the press, adding, 'Don't you think Mrs Prime has been through enough?' It made not the slightest difference.

Once again we had to resort to hiding in the barristers' robing room. I sat on one of the metal lockers in there, while a taxi was hailed and brought to a back door. Then we made our getaway. I ducked as a few cameramen came running towards the taxi but we were soon well clear of them and on our way to the Temple, and to Mr Carman's chambers, where we were served with tea. Our host and Mr Clover were concerned, sympathetic and helpful and I appreciated their advice, but just then I wanted to get back to Cheltenham.

Outside the Temple, Mr Davies hailed a taxi which took us first to Charing Cross. There Jean said goodbye, alighted and went to catch a train back to her home, while we were driven on to where Geoff's solicitor had parked his car.

At last I was on my way home. As Mr Davies negotiated the London rush-hour traffic, I sat in the passenger seat – caught in the backlash of the day's events.

The appeal and its outcome had been far worse than I could possibly have imagined.

'You've nothing to lose,' people had kept telling us beforehand, but right now I felt we had lost everything.

Once again I had had to sit in utter frustration and humiliation as Geoff's offences had been proclaimed and his character and motives given the worst possible interpretation. Once again we had been, and would continue to be, exposed before the eyes of the world. And in the end that utterly unthinkable sentence had been upheld. British justice had evidently spoken its last crushing word.

Suddenly, over the car radio came the impassive voice of the newsreader, giving details of the appeal. Horror-struck, I wondered how Geoff would be hearing the news. My heart ached for him and for the boys and my parents.

I tried to imagine their reactions. Mark and Stephen would probably bottle up their feelings. Craig would be bewildered as well as sad, having prayed so earnestly that God would reduce Geoff's sentence. I felt too devastated myself to know how best to help him or anyone else, but I wanted to be with them and try to share their pain at least.

At my parents' home, the boys and I were reunited – and there were many tears. Mine didn't ease the weight of grief and bitter disappointment that I was carrying.

Next morning I saw Jane briefly – long enough for her to realise how bad I felt. In the afternoon, having been given a special visit to see Geoff, I went with a very heavy heart to Long Lartin.

When my husband and I were together I broke down and cried. Between sobs I said, 'Forgive me, Geoff. I'm so sorry about all this. I really believed the sentence would be cut. And now I'm no help to you at all.'

He put his arm round me and called me by a pet name which he'd sometimes used.

'You've comforted me often enough,' he said. 'It's about time I did the same for you. I didn't expect anything from this appeal, whereas you did. It would have been better if you hadn't had such high hopes.'

He told me how he had heard the news. As he'd been going down to tea at half-past four the assistant governor had called him into his office. There he had been told, baldly, that his appeal had been dismissed. In speaking to him, the assistant governor had used a calm matter-of-fact tone of voice, and had then said he could go and have his tea. Apparently this was standard procedure with appeals.

Geoff said, 'We're back to hanging on by our finger nails.' It was a phrase he had often used. I couldn't seem to stop crying and he went on trying to comfort me, using another favourite phrase of his – one that he would quote in difficult times: 'One more time, Rhona.'

Just before leaving, still in tears, I pleaded, 'Don't blame me, Geoff.'

'Daft mop,' he said, hugging me. 'One day we'll walk up Cleeve Hill together again.'

I left, amazed by his attitude. I, on the other hand, seemed to be swimming in blackness.

God seemed to have withdrawn from me and I was filled with doubts. Had everything I'd said and done so far been utterly wrong? If not, why had this happened?

I felt drained. Cooking a meal or even climbing the stairs seemed like impossible feats. One day I couldn't even face getting out of bed. A great weight seemed to be pressing down on me.

For once my friends seemed strangely silent and I felt too resentful to ring them or go to any meeting at which I might meet them.

Then, on Sunday afternoon, Jane called.

'I can't cope,' I told her, defeatedly.

'You can, you must and you will,' she told me with her customary forthrightness, adding, 'You've got God. You must have or you would certainly have had a breakdown by now.'

I thought, *That's easy to say!* But her words began to have a bracing effect.

Members of my family and some other friends started to phone or visit – to listen, comfort, help and pray. I decided to go along to a meeting. June was there and came over to chat.

After a while, she said, 'Rhona, there's something I think I should share with you. I couldn't tell you before, but now I think it's right to do so. We were praying with some friends about the appeal a few days before the proceedings. One of the people there was the person who'd been leading the meeting – a real man of God.' She mentioned his name and I recognised it, having been present at other meetings he had led.

Then she went on, 'While we were praying he said, "The appeal won't work." He'd seen in his mind a pair of chained hands which, he believed, symbolised God's hands and the fact that they were tied showed that God could not act because Geoff had not yet repented before him.'

Her words struck me forcibly. As I was recovering, she said, 'It's awful, isn't it? But at least we know how to pray now.'

'I think you're right,' I said, thoughtfully. Geoff had been repentant and remorseful before men, I believed, but not yet before God. I saw more clearly than ever that his only hope lay – as did mine and everyone else's – in being humble and broken before God. So that, above all, was what we had to pray for.

I felt open to God again. As the meeting continued, different people spoke to me, each giving me some hope or encouragement. Then God gave me a deep experience of himself. Afterwards, I was more than ever aware that he was with me all the time, helping me to press on in spite of physical exhaustion and emotional and mental turmoil.

It was impossible not to keep going over and over in my mind and in conversation with friends the appeal and the trial before it.

Why had Geoff been labelled as utterly ruthless and rational when, as Mr Carman had so clearly pointed out, so many aspects of his personality and behaviour did not tally with that description? As far as I could see, the psychiatric reports had been completely disregarded. Wouldn't a totally ruthless and rational person have destroyed all the evidence and run away? Was the making of a full confession before trial and sentence the act of such a man?

And why the mention of Admiral Byng? Even after finding

out that he was an eighteenth century admiral shot, possibly unjustly, for alleged cowardice in war, I was none the wiser. What did such a man have to do with a twentieth century peacetime spy?

And what about the whole espionage business? Wasn't there hypocrisy involved in that? If spying was wrong, and I certainly believed that it was, then it was wrong for everyone, no matter whom one was spying for or against.

Why hadn't other spies been given similar treatment? Anthony Blunt for example? He had spied for the Russians for a far longer period of time than had my husband; had enjoyed many more privileges and accepted far higher responsibilities – including membership of MI5; had been involved with other spies – some of whom he'd helped to defect; had been active in wartime as well as in peace; and had consistently denied his espionage activities until 1964, more than thirty years after he'd begun working for the Russians, when he'd agreed to confess and give information in return for immunity.

It was from a newspaper obituary to this man that I learnt these details. The article ended with the words: 'At any rate he was, on his public exposure, dealt with comparatively leniently, with the annulling of his knighthood of the Royal Victorian Order.'

Comparatively leniently indeed! I thought wrathfully. Anthony Blunt lost his knighthood, and my husband – from a much lowlier social background and work situation, spying in peacetime, alone and for a shorter period of time, and having made a full confession – was given thirty-five years! Was such a sentence just? And how could it be compatible with the claim that credit had been given to him for his detailed confession?

Evidently my friends and I were not alone in raising such questions or in the conclusions we reached about them. On *Any Questions* one day a questioner asked the panel whether they felt that justice had been done in my husband's case. Some of the speakers said forcefully that they believed it had not been and the audience resoundingly applauded them.

Then there was the letter to the *Guardian* newspaper on May 2nd.

Sir, How does Lord Justice Lawton know what 'right-minded members of the public' think (*Guardian*, April 22)? I am as certain that I am right-minded as he is certain that he is, and I do not believe that Geoffrey Prime should have been sentenced to thirty-eight years imprisonment. I don't think anyone should be sentenced for that long.

Mr Prime was convicted of sexual offences for which he received a three-year sentence. It is generally agreed that prison is an inappropriate way of treating or punishing a sexual offender; it is, I suppose, a woeful admission that we cannot do anything better. However, most right-minded people would no doubt agree that certain individuals suffered as a result of these offences, and that therefore they are abhorrent acts.

Spying is a different matter, beset with moral ambiguities. Evidently, the powers-that-be recognise the problem. If the spies are rich and well-connected then they are treated circumspectly. But if poor and inadequate they are treated with extraordinary severity. It is not clear that a single individual has suffered as a result of Prime's spying activities, yet he is to spend thirty-five years in prison. Do right-minded people really support this cruelty?

Most shameful of all is the case of Mrs Prime who made the difficult decision to tell the police about her husband. Implicit in her action was the belief that her husband would be treated with justice, that his punishment would be fair, and that he would be helped.

                                                Karen Hewitt

The letter echoed my own troubled feelings about what had happened. I was troubled, too, about the *way* things had been done. What was it all about? Why all the rush and subsequent intolerable escalating pressure and tension of bringing the trial forward? And why only five months between that and the appeal? Surely that was far too short a gap, given the extraordinary publicity surrounding the case? Wasn't it more usual for people serving long sentences to have an appeal not months but years after the trial, when there would be less danger of massive media coverage and all the possible complications and pressures arising from this?

And then there were the *in camera* proceedings. Necessary as they may have been they raised other questions in my mind. Had Mr Carman really been able, in the circumstances, to examine and assess thoroughly the evidence presented by the Security Services – evidence which would surely have been highly technical? Or did he have to accept at face value what he was shown and told?

While I mulled over these matters, the press coverage of every aspect and angle of the story continued. Articles ranged from those on security matters in general to those on Geoff in particular, or people dragged up from his past.

What have we set in motion? I wondered, horrified. Would the spate of articles and stories never come to an end?

At least some of the rumours currently circulating were checked by the publication in May of the Report of the Security Commission. In essence, its findings were that those responsible for carrying out security procedures did not deserve blame though the procedures themselves needed to be re-examined. The report suggested that polygraphic and psychological tests should be looked into; that random searches of staff leaving GCHQ, and perhaps other government establishments, should be introduced; and that for positive vetting individuals should be required to allow access to their medical records.

With so much coverage being given to these matters, it was natural that I should keep thinking and talking about them. But doing so often caused me to feel overwhelmed, or to harbour doubt, resentment and other negative attitudes. These attitudes, as well as my many unanswered questions, I had to learn to keep handing over to God, asking him to deal with them, with the situation and with me.

I needed to take the same action when people hurt or annoyed me. Chief among these were those who caused me to feel rejected or unclean. Their unspoken message to me seemed to be, 'We're good people. Don't contaminate us.' They appeared to be afraid that I would become tainted or would taint them through going to prison to see Geoff.

My own thinking on the matter was greatly clarified on the day I heard a preacher speaking on 'guilt by association'. There were some Christians, he said, who didn't get involved for fear of becoming or being dubbed as guilty by association with evil. Yet, he pointed out, it was often in dark situations that Christians and the Christian message were most needed.

I couldn't have agreed more – and thought of the example of Jesus who, though perfect, mixed with outcasts and wrongdoers: hating the sin but loving the sinner.

We had long been awaiting the Press Council's reply regarding the article in the *News of the World*.

In the summer, after a happy family holiday in France – made possible through the generosity of friends – I was greeted with some shattering news. In our absence Geoff had been informed that his complaint about the article had been rejected. In essence, the ruling of the council was that Geoff's solicitors had failed to satisfy them that the allegations in the story were false.

Feeling sick at heart, I went to see Geoff who was understandably wild at the outcome. The Press Council's judgment, he said, had been a perverse one. Had the allegations been true they would surely have been highlighted in the report of the Security Commission in May.

We were outraged, but helpless. Bringing a libel action against the paper would involve extensive and lengthy investigations in Britain and America and we were not in a position to make them ourselves or to pay anyone else to do so – legal aid not being available for libel actions.

So Geoff – unjustly, I believe – sank lower in people's estimation and we all had to bear the repercussions and the knowledge that what had happened could have a detrimental effect on parole discussions at some future date.

Knowing that people could virtually say what they liked

about us, since we had no effective form of redress, made us feel very vulnerable. I could now sympathise deeply with people in similar situations, particularly those who felt completely alone and powerless.

I was fortunate in that after the appeal, as after the trial, kind supportive letters flooded in. Then too, I had the opportunity to put into print what I believed to be the truth about all that had happened. Above all, I was completely certain that our lives were in God's hands and that I could trust him to be completely just and fair, while working everything out for the good of those who love him.

My husband, supported by few people and having no such faith, found it increasingly difficult not to become cynical and depressed.

28

Where is your God now?

'Where is your God now?'

Geoff put the question to me after the appeal in one of his more bitter moments. His attitude to religion in general and Christianity in particular was at this time rather equivocal.

'You have been optimistic all along,' he continued. 'You said that if we told the truth it'd go in our favour. But how can anyone say that it did? You felt sure that the trial would go well and then the appeal. But where has all this truth-telling got us?'

I had no pat answers for him because, humanly speaking, honesty does not in our case appear to have been the *best* policy, though I still believe and know that it's the *right* one.

'All I can say, Geoff,' I replied, 'is that I'm having to learn that God doesn't always answer our prayers in the way that we want him to. But I know he has heard us and that it will be for the best in the end. You could never come out of here a whole person if we hadn't done what we did.'

His response was quite different this time.

'I can't agree with you there,' he said. 'How can I come out of this place a whole person? I can see daily reminders of the effects of long prison sentences.'

I didn't doubt what he said – probation officers and others having told me of the dehumanising, demoralising effects of long-term prison sentences.

'We should have done it a different way,' he said, adding, 'Don't get me wrong. I don't blame you at all for what you did. You did what you had to do and I will never hold it against you. But if we had done things differently, we'd have been better off, I'm sure. I should have remained silent until after the trial.'

Looked at from a human standpoint, Geoff was right, I thought. We were fools to ourselves. Had we been more calculating and canny, we might well have less to bear.

So where *is* my God in all this?

He is in the situation – in this twisting, tangled, mysterious way of toil and tears: 'closer than breathing, nearer than hands and feet'.

Sometimes he makes his presence and help very real and obvious.

Once, when Craig's birthday was coming up and I had no money to give him a decent birthday tea or present, I received a letter and a cheque for twenty pounds from someone I'd never met – a friend of a friend, who'd suddenly felt prompted to send us a gift.

I was overjoyed and very grateful, and we were able to have a happy birthday with Craig.

On my next visit to Long Lartin, I told Geoff what had happened. His reaction was a very puzzled, 'But you must know the person who sent you the money.'

'I don't,' I assured him. 'That's what Christians are like. They care about people they don't know personally and are prompted to do these things by God who knows about our needs.'

Never having experienced that kind of love or that kind of God, he couldn't understand it.

On another occasion, due to a misunderstanding regarding Social Security, finances ran very low. Just then a bill arrived and I started worrying about how I was going to pay it. This was still very much on my mind when I went to a meeting. Afterwards, in talking to the speaker, I mentioned the matter.

'God gives us all we need,' he said. 'So how much do you need?'

'A hundred pounds,' I answered.

'Then that's what we'll pray for,' he said – and did.

'Now,' he continued, 'keep thanking God for answering that prayer – and don't stop.'

The next morning, I thanked God that he was going to answer our prayer. I did the same the second morning, and the third. But as one day succeeded another and nothing happened except that our financial situation worsened, my faith was strained to the limit. Still, albeit faint-heartedly, I continued to thank God.

On the eleventh day an envelope came through the post. It had my name on it but having been misaddressed, it had been to two other places before being delivered at our house.

I tore open the flap and pulled out the contents. The envelope contained five twenty pound notes, and nothing else.

I stared at them, moved to the depth of my being. By this time I had started work again with the School Meals' Service, so I had to hurry out and drive myself to school. My progress that morning was probably none too steady, due to the tears in my eyes!

Geoff was very struck by this story when I related it to him; at the same time he didn't really know what to make of it all.

But it wasn't only through gifts of money that God showed me how close and caring he was.

Changing the car battery is one of the extra jobs I've had to learn to do since Geoff was taken away – and not one that I enjoy at all, either. Once when I was trying to do this, nothing seemed to go right and I grew more and more angry and upset.

Then the telephone rang and I went into the house to answer it.

The caller was someone from Cornwall: a friend, but one who doesn't contact me often, nor I her.

'Are you all right, Rhona?' she asked. 'I was praying for you when I suddenly felt I should ring you.'

'No, I'm not all right,' I replied, but already I felt better, knowing that God cared about my struggles and frustration and had prompted a friend to ring. We had a good talk and then, with her wise, loving words ringing in my ears, I went back to complete the job – without much trouble.

Then there was the shower. We had had it installed for reasons of economy and convenience a few years earlier.

One day it stopped working. Someone who looked at it said he thought it might cost rather a lot of money to have it repaired. Finances were once again low, so I thought, *I'm going to pray about this!*

I told God, very reverently, that we needed the shower unit working properly as we couldn't afford baths or the money for repairs.

To my astonishment I'm ashamed to say, and joy, the shower started working again. That was in February. A year later, as I type these words, it's still working.

But these are the highlights – very few and precious. God does not always answer prayers or intervene like that. Unlike Paul Snow's my car, for instance, does not respond to prayer, however earnest and heartfelt!

So where is my God when prayers are apparently unanswered and the going is tough and the future unknown? He's still with me, hearing my prayers but withholding the answers or replying in ways which I didn't expect, for his own very good reasons, and ready to help and guide me.

And what he is doing *in* me is just as important as what he is doing *for* me. He is slowly changing my attitudes to people and things.

I am learning not to be so bound by possessions and to worry less about material things. People and relationships matter far more, and God gives us all we need – although not necessarily all we want.

God is teaching me, too, that true freedom, no matter what our outward circumstances may be, is only to be found in living for him.

Above all he is teaching me to love people with the forgiving, caring practical love that he, perfectly and continually, shows towards me. It is only as I receive that love that I'm able to love God, Geoff and others more and more each day.

Increasingly I realise that God's love is for everyone, including those 'forgotten people' whom society puts behind bars. I have been made very aware of the lives of these people and am catching a vision of what God could do amongst them.

Geoff is changing too, and our relationship, amazingly, is deepening. He admits that he used to be so wrapped up in his problems that he was often hardly aware of his surroundings or even of us. Now he is growing in understanding of me, as I of him.

'At times I can see the hurt in your eyes,' he said once. 'I realise that it was there sometimes before but I didn't care to notice it. All those wasted years when I never really looked into your eyes!'

He told me that during the last months before his arrest he'd spent hours driving aimlessly about in the car, unable to concentrate on anything because of his tortured state of mind.

Now, though facing what has been described as a sentence without hope, he is determined to keep his mind active, and hopes to start a course of study with the Open University.

We both continue to press for the psychological help which we believe he needs and which he has been wanting all along. The espionage business took precedence over everything else for a while but now, perhaps, something can be done. Unfortunately, through not working in the same Health Authority area as Long Lartin, Dr Marks cannot continue to see Geoff. Another psychiatrist has talked with him but at present obstacles still exist to the treatment identified as necessary by Dr Marks.

I feel sad about this, as I do about the fact that Mr Glass, who is not only a very spiritual person, but also a politically aware one, has never managed to visit my husband. He applied for a pastoral visit in January but six months later when – sadly from our point of view – he was called to a different congregation, he had not received the necessary permission.

The boys and my mother continue to be supportive to

Geoff, keeping in touch with him through letters, cards and occasional visits. A few other warm-hearted people also write to him.

Craig is growing as a Christian. He, like me, is having to learn to cope at times with big disappointments, such as the outcome of the appeal; and smaller ones, such as the disappearance in May of our cat Pushka and her continuing absence despite earnest prayer. Stephen and Mark are open to discussion about our Christian faith and I know that God loves them and have many proofs that he is protecting them in the midst of all the dangers and temptations which face our young people today.

Life continues to be hard in many ways for us all. What my mother and I were told separately about five years ago has proved and is proving true. Things certainly did go wrong in my life and I did, eventually, turn back, wholeheartedly, to God.

As for the long dark tunnel of which we were also told, I believe I entered that after the trial and am still struggling through it, while seeing some glimpses of light ahead and holding on to many hands and hand-holds along the way – these being God's promises and all the help, good things and wonderful friends that he gives me.

One special promise was given to me after the appeal. Someone at a meeting I attended wanted me to take particular note of some words in the Bible. They came in the book of Joel, which I knew very little about, and they were: 'I will repay you for the years which the locusts have eaten.'

Hearing them I was filled with joy, convinced that God was really speaking to me.

I told Geoff about this verse and the incident. He was very struck by the words and wanted to know where they came from so that he could read them for himself in his Bible.

Later, I went to a small prayer group of the Prison Christian Fellowship, at which members shared their needs and prayed for each other. Suddenly, moved almost to tears, I heard someone praying for my husband – asking God to repay him for the years which the locusts had eaten.

I now feel very much that this is our verse and that God is already bringing good out of our seemingly tragic situation and that he will continue to do so.

At present I am back with the School Meals' Service, my job wonderfully having been kept open for me for a whole year. I have also been doing voluntary probation work and perhaps more opportunities will arise in this field or in connection with the Prison Christian Fellowship. One thing I would dearly love to do, if it ever became possible, is to open a Christian coffee-cum-bookshop, which I feel would meet a growing need in our community. Of course God might have some quite different ideas about my future! All I can be sure of is that his plans for me, Geoff, the boys and everyone else are best, because with God nothing is impossible and his knowledge of each of us is total and his love for us – limitless.

I sense that Geoff is also coming to believe this. In a recent letter to me he wrote, 'I believe that with God's help and your love I can scale any peak and find true peace in my heart.'

I thank God that he brought me to the point of turning to him and putting my life – past, present and future – completely into his hands; and now my constant prayer is that, just as Geoff's trial is my trial, my God will truly become his God, so that he can write the best possible ending to our story.